GRACE IN
ADDICTION

GRACE IN ADDICTION

The Good News of Alcoholics
Anonymous for Everybody

JOHN Z.

MOCKINGBIRD

MOCKINGBIRD

Copyright © 2012 by Mockingbird Ministries
Mockingbird Ministries
100 West Jefferson Street
Charlottesville, VA 22902
www.mbird.com

ALL RIGHTS RESERVED.

No part of this book may be used or reproduced in any manner whatsoever without written permission, except in the case of brief quotations embodied in critical articles or reviews.

Cover design by Stephanie Fishwick. Editing and book design by William McDavid. Published 2012 and printed by Createspace.com in the United States of America.

ISBN-13: 978-1479313815

ISBN-10: 1479313815

DISCLAIMER

MOCKINGBIRD MINISTRIES ("MOCKINGBIRD") IS AN INDEPENDENT NOT-FOR-PROFIT MINISTRY SEEKING TO CONNECT, COMMENT UPON AND EXPLORE THE CHRISTIAN FAITH WITH AND THROUGH CONTEMPORARY CULTURE. MOCKINGBIRD FULLY DISCLAIMS ANY SPONSORSHIP, ASSOCIATION, OR CONNECTION WITH ALCOHOLICS ANONYMOUS ("AA"). LIKEWISE, MOCKINGBIRD HAS NO AFFILIATION, SPONSORSHIP OR CONNECTION WITH ANY OF THE AUTHOR(S), ARTIST(S) OR PUBLICATIONS QUOTED OR REFERENCED HEREIN. THE CONTENT IS INTENDED FOR THE PURPOSE OF COMMENTARY, STUDY, DISCUSSION, AND LITERARY OR RELIGIOUS CRITIQUE. FINALLY, MOCKINGBIRD DISCLAIMS ANY AFFILIATION, SPONSORSHIP OR CONNECTION WITH ANY OTHER ENTITY USING THE WORDS "MOCKINGBIRD" AND "MINISTRIES" ALONE OR IN COMBINATION

This book is dedicated to Chuck T. of Cleveland/Danville, Ohio (1933 – 2006). The quintessential AA sage, half rapscallion and half genius, Chuck was born (a twin) in Akron, Ohio, AA's birthplace. Due to severe dyslexia, he did not learn to read until he was 35. He sobered up in Cleveland, "the cradle of AA", and spent much of his sobriety working in the Holy Family Home as a nurse, providing hospice like care to the greater Cleveland area. On one occasion, he met Bill W, AA's famous founder. Chuck retired to a house at the end of a dirt road in rural Danville, Ohio, surrounded by Amish neighbors. He attended thousands of AA meetings, started groups in Cleveland and Mount Vernon, and helped countless members of AA find sobriety. I have never met a wiser, more insightful counselor. He died with 39 years of sobriety His obituary stated accurately: "He helped many people, and was loved by many."

Acknowledgements

This book was born out of a talk given at the 2009 NYC Mockingbird Conference at Calvary/St. George's Episcopal Church, where AA co-founder Sam Shoemaker served as Rector in the 1930s. A second talk, given at the 2010 M'bird Conference in Pensacola, also influenced the book.

Without the effort and encouragement of Mockingbird's team, a full-length version of GIA never would have come to fruition. In particular, the incredibly gifted Will McDavid has been invaluable to the creation of this book, serving tirelessly as my editor and sounding board. Enough thanks cannot be offered to him for his insight and patience. David Zahl, too, gave up endless hours of his time in helping to shape and improve the work.

Tom B helped me to put these ideas together, and many of them originate from conversations we have shared over our many years of friendship.

Similarly, my family have given much of themselves (including sweat and graying hair) to the shaping of this material as it has played out in our lives together. We are so blessed to have each other, a family of advocates, second to none I know.

The Women of The Cathedral Church of the Advent in Birmingham, Alabama were thoughtful enough to support this work from the moment of its conception. Likewise, huge thanks are due to the wonderful people of Holy Cross, Sullivan's Island, who allowed me to test out this material on them, week in and week out over the past five years.

I have been fortunate to experience expressions of AA in Ohio, Alabama, New York City, Oxford, England, and Charleston, South Carolina. In each place I have met life-saving friends, sponsors, sponsees, and many of the people I most respect in this world. "The Kenyon Hellraisers" deserve singular mention for, among other things, driving me to all of my first meetings.

And finally, there are the two most special people of all, my wife and daughter. D is a constant example of beauty and grace, while Little D has become my muse. Her anticipated arrival prompted me to write each day for the 7 months that ultimately led to her birth. The result is this book…and a very happy father.

Contents

Acknowledgments		7
Introduction		11
The Twelve Steps		19

Part I.   Shaving the Enemy

Step 1	Admitted We Were Powerless	31
Step 2	Came to Believe	53
Step 3	Made a Decision	61

Part II.   The Heart of the Matter

Step 4	Made a Searching and Fearless Moral Inventory of Ourselves	83
Step 5	Admitted to God, to Ourselves, And to Another Human Being	115
Step 6	Were Entirely Ready	125
Step 7	Humbly Asked	141
Step 8	Became Willing to Make Amends	165
Step 9	Made Direct Amends	175

Part III.   Growing Into Grace

Step 10	Continued to Take Personal Inventory	195
Step 11	Conscious Contact	209
Step 12	Having Had a Spiritual Awakening	223

Conclusion   239

Epilogue	257
Appendix I: Mortimers and Lulus	265
Appendix II: Mingling with Alcohol in Sobriety	271
Appendix III: The Serenity Prayer	277

Introduction

On a Friday night in late 2011, in a small nightclub in Charleston, South Carolina, I witnessed a crowd's exuberant reaction when the DJ put on an old disco record called "I Don't Want to Be a Freak (But I Can't Help Myself)" by Dynasty. With its whispering voices, infectious funky hook and sizzling Cuban percussion, the track sounded amazing. The crowd of dancers gathered on the floor practically exploded with enthusiasm the moment the chorus circled back around. Onlookers rushed to join the frenzy. Soon the entire group of more than fifty club-goers was singing along to the refrain *en masse* with their arms raised in the air: "I don't wanna be a freak, but I can't help-my-self…I don't wanna be a freak, but I can't help-my-self…"

"I Don't Want to Be a Freak" was recorded in Los Angeles in 1979 at the height of the disco craze. That same year it reached #20 in the UK Singles charts. Not long after that, disco took a serious nosedive in the US, becoming the epitome of un-cool. Yet here we were, more than 30 years later in the Southern Low Country, very far from Los Angeles and even further from London, and this little record was finding a second wind. It may have been one of many disco tracks played that night, but "I Don't Want to Be a Freak" stood out because of the crescendo reaction it received from the primarily twenty-something audience.

A few interesting things were going on in that little moment. First, an old song was finding fresh life with a whole new generation of dancers. The song was as much their song in the 21st century as it had been their parents' in the late 1970s. Second, the lyrical content made an impression. The inability to help oneself seems hardly an appropriate occasion for conviviality. *But these young people were connecting with a seemingly downbeat message with a surprising amount of eagerness, the result of which, surprisingly, was joy and dancing – the thing that one associates with celebration and freedom.*

I see this same dynamic at play in the world of twelve-step recovery. In owning their defeat—through the infamous 1st Step: *"We admitted we were powerless…that our lives had become unmanageable"*– defeated people find a pathway to hope, freedom, and exuberant joy. A tragic diagnosis opens the door to all of the things that its verdict seemed to deny. As Bill Wilson, founder of Alcoholics Anonymous, wrote in 1955, "The principle that we shall find no enduring strength until we first admit complete defeat is the main taproot from which our whole society has sprung and flowered." Alcoholics Anonymous and the various recovery programs it has spawned display a practical spirituality whose fruits are undeniable and far-reaching. Their insights are worthy of study.

The peculiarity of AA's approach is apparent right from the outset, its foundation being an ever-unpopular skepticism concerning human willpower. David Brooks drew attention to this aspect of Alcoholics Anonymous in a 2010 New York Times editorial entitled *"Bill Wilson's Gospel"*: "In a culture that generally celebrates empowerment and self-esteem, AA begins with disempowerment. The goal is to get people to gain control over their lives, but it all begins with an act of surrender and an admission of weakness."

I have been reflecting upon these matters since becoming a member of AA in 1996 during my freshmen year of college, following a three-week stay in an in-patient rehabilitative hospital in West Georgia.

"I'm Also a Member" (Hair Club for Men)

I started drinking and smoking pot when I was 12. I was a typical pothead teenager, full of artistic inclinations and rebellious temperament. I remember arguing with my mother after I was pulled aside for a security check at an airport in Stuttgart. Never mind the fact that I had my hair in pigtails and was sporting a T-shirt that featured a three-eyed, three-eared, one-legged Mickey Mouse – who did they think they were, judging a book by its cover?! They don't know me! Of course, I now see that they were looking in the right place if they wanted to keep drug paraphernalia off of their airplanes.

In getting drunk and high I found short-term relief from all of the confusion that I now associate with my experience of puberty. I was a late bloomer and felt especially insecure. The fact that my father was living in Europe for a stint, which led to my having to attend three different high schools, probably exacerbated the situation. But the taste for excess seemed be in my blood from the very beginning. It is probably worth noting that my family tree is spattered with the wreckage of a long line of alcoholism.

Despite my behavior and the damage it caused, getting into trouble was never very effective in dissuading me from abusing. If anything, it inspired me to be more crafty and deceitful. My loyalty, first and foremost, was to escapism in the form of mind-altering substances. They soon became a necessity: a self-prescribed medication, or at least a requirement for coping in an oppressive world. Not surprisingly, I soon experienced suspensions from school, an arrest, legal trouble, and the complete collapse of my relationship with my family. On my senior yearbook page, I included a photo of myself leaning my head against a trash can, along with the following quote from The Cure: "The further I get from the things that I care about, the less I care about how much further away I get."

I was full of blame, convinced that everyone was conspiring against me. Perhaps school was my problem. After a three-month hiatus in Bolivia, however, I absurdly concluded that my problem was not so much school, but rather the United States of America.

A year later, on the way to my intervention, I told my mother that, "if everyone would just leave me alone, I'd be okay!" It was less than 24 hours later, in the confines of a hospital bed, that it occurred to me for the first time that I had gotten way off track. "How is it," I wondered, "that I've gotten to the point that I love drugs and alcohol more than my own mother?" These and other similar thoughts led me into the world of AA – kicking and screaming, but beaten nonetheless. As an AA newcomer once said, "I'm giving up fun forever." I could sympathize.

And so began my journey into the world of recovery through the Twelve Steps. "You don't slide in on a rainbow" is another AA adage that proved true.

Four years of sobriety later, and in wake of a painful breakup, this same journey led me back into the Church. At one of the initial services I attended, I remember reading for the first time in over ten years the words of confession from the *Book of Common*

Prayer. "We have erred and strayed from Thy ways like lost sheep. We have followed too much the devices and desires of our own hearts." I remembered the lines from my childhood. I remembered how abstract and irrelevant the whole religious endeavor had seemed to me in my youth. But now, in that low moment, I found in them a more complete understanding of myself than I had known in years. It was another crucial moment for me, the beginning of a re-conversion. And it was my experience of sobriety in AA that paved the way for me to connect the dots between my life and Christianity.

In keeping with the aforementioned extremist tendencies, if I was going to become a Christian, then I was going all the way. After three years of seminary at Oxford, I was ordained to the ministry in 2007. I continue to participate in the fellowship of Alcoholics Anonymous.

Strangers Are Just Friends Who Haven't Met Yet

The world of AA closely resembles a church. People from all different backgrounds gather together on a regular basis. Prayer is encouraged. Many of the members talk about God, how He has changed their lives and enabled them to do that which they could never have done before. Plus, in AA there is an obvious social energy. Long-standing friendships are often formed. Alcoholics Anonymous offers a massive support network, has no fees, and hugely emphasizes outreach. It all sounds suspiciously familiar.

The recovery community, however, is often quick to distance itself from "organized religion." While AA meetings may resemble religious services, it is stated at the outset of every meeting that "AA is not allied with any sect, denomination, politics, organization or institution…" So while it may function in the lives of its members in a way that looks like church, the idea that it actually *is church* is staunchly denied. This train of thought has roots extending all the way back to its earliest days. The goal was and is to avoid controversy at all costs, for the sake of unity. Thus, AA has only one officially stated purpose: helping alcoholics to find sobriety. Such driving instincts have given AA an opportunity to blossom and thrive in a world where similar endeavors often fail.

In moving from AA into the Christian Church, I have nevertheless been surprised to see how well the two do in fact relate to each other. At their best, the two have so much to teach each other. The AA text that deals with the 11th Step is especially positive on involvement with religious institutions, but that aspect of the literature is rarely mentioned.

The wall of separation between AA and the Christian Church is unfortunate. It's as though they are looking at each other from across the street, assuming the worst about each other, rather than hoping they might become friends. I hope this book will serve to help build such a bridge, or at least reveal that this apparent disconnect is ultimately insubstantial.

I am not the first to attempt to wed the worlds of Christianity and Twelve Step recovery. A well-known example called "Celebrate Recovery" started at Rick Warren's (author of *The Purpose Driven Life*) Saddleback Church. It now runs in churches all over America and greatly resembles other Twelve Step groups. Unfortunately, like many Christian approaches to addiction, this program often contains an excessively optimistic view of the believer's ability to move towards God.[1] In doing so, it has unwittingly undone the entire foundation of the 1st Step –

---

[1] Another popular book on Christianity and the Twelve Steps is *A Hunger for Healing* by J. Keith Miller, and it exhibits problems similar to those of "Celebrate Recovery."

admission of total powerlessness – upon which the world of recovery is built.

Yet there are Christian theological traditions that begin with a realistic view of human nature. These traditions begin, at least in theory, with an emphasis on the comprehensive nature of human limitation and sin, and as such they are often better equipped to speak about addiction in general, and AA in particular.[2] But for whatever reason, as far as I'm aware, none have done so. This present work seeks to take a step in that direction, showing how AA buys into an understanding of human nature that has, for the most part, been lost in both secular and sacred spheres.

My thesis is simple: *AA and traditional Reformation Christianity make sense of life in a way that is relevant to every person.* I have tried to show what this angle on life actually looks like, how it views the world, and how it changes a person for the better.

It may surprise many AAs to discover that there are churches that actually agree with them about the nature of life in God's world. They might also be surprised to hear that AA actually inherited much of its worldview directly from Christianity. Conversely, many Christians may find that familiarizing themselves with old-fashioned Protestant theology, as it's brilliantly expressed in AA, will enrich and deepen their own self-understanding. Like Dynasty's hit from 1979, we hope that a great song from the past will find a second life in the pages of this book and in the hearts and minds of its readers.

Finally, it is my sincere hope that this material will even inspire you to try working the Twelve Steps for yourself. In the

---

[2] This is true especially of the denominations rooted in the Protestant Reformation, such as the Presbyterian Church, the Lutheran Church, and formative strands of the Anglican Communion. Such denominations openly acknowledge the primary problem of the "bound will" in the individual, and they view humans, apart from being moved by God, as incapable of choosing the things necessary for their salvation. For them, faith comes as a gift and not an individual choice.

chapters that involve taking particular actions (such as steps 3, 4, 9, and 10), I have tried my best to offer clear directions on how to do the associated work.

When my parents placed me in pre-school at Calvary Episcopal Church in Manhattan in the late 70s, they had no idea that they were exposing me to the roots of AA.[3] I did not choose my college because it was located just a few miles from the birthplace of AA in Ohio, although it was. Pure coincidence perhaps, but also perhaps not. And then there's the fact that I am now ordained in a traditional Protestant denomination, as well as a grateful member of AA. It occurs to me that I am positioned, even uniquely so, to comment on the myriad points of connection between Christianity and AA. Indeed, "I can't help-my-self."

Please do not be discouraged if you find some of the initial material to be off-putting. Given a chance, you may soon find that it inspires the spiritual equivalent of dancing. You might even do well to wonder if the DJ mentioned at the beginning of this section was yours truly.

I lift my cup of coffee to you,

JAZ+
Charleston, South Carolina
June 11, 2012

---

[3] Calvary Episcopal Church's rector in the 1930s was Sam Shoemaker, Bill Wilson's dear friend and advisor. It was in Shoemaker's office that Steps 4 – 9 were first written down.

The Twelve Steps

"AA's Twelve Steps are a group of principles, spiritual in their nature, which, if practiced as a way of life, can expel the obsession to drink and enable the sufferer to become happily and usefully whole…Many people, nonalcoholics, report that as a result of the practice of AA's Twelve Steps, they have been able to meet other difficulties of life. They think that the Twelve Steps can mean more than sobriety for problem drinkers. They see in them a way to happy and effective living for many, alcoholic or not"[4]

The problem of addiction compels any observer to re-examine her view of human nature and, consequently, God. Things that seem to be true for the addict often challenge and contradict our comfortable assumptions about reality. Indeed, addiction presents an impasse that must be reckoned with. Its victims are countless and most treatments have little long-term impact. Alcoholics

---

[4] Bill Wilson, *Twelve Steps and Twelve Traditions* (New York: AA World Services, 1953), 15. This book makes use of two main texts for AA: *Twelve Steps and Twelve Traditions*, abbreviated *"12 & 12"*, and *Alcoholics Anonymous*, abbreviated "Big Book." Unless otherwise noted, citations will be from the Big Book.

Anonymous and the Twelve Steps represent one of the only rays of hope on an otherwise dark horizon, having consistently helped turn around truly devastated lives. It is not surprising that courts and schools continue to mandate that addicts attend Twelve Step programs; their success is undeniable.

The success of AA cannot be divorced from its core understanding of human beings and their need for God. Indeed, the Twelve Step approach is based on claims about the relationship between God and man, claims which may be implicit in Christianity but are not usually stressed in so singular a fashion.

Of course, Christianity is significantly more complicated than AA and carries with it 2000 years of history – and corresponding baggage. AA is less than 80 years old. Imagine a grandfather sitting with his 2-year-old granddaughter. She can only say few words, and while directly descended from him, her picture of life is simpler and fresher by comparison. Such is the relationship of AA to Christianity. For whatever reason, the basics of faith that are stressed in every meeting of AA do not usually seem to govern or characterize modern day church life.

The chief concern of Twelve Step recovery is redemption, pure and simple. The sober alcoholic who has found joyful release from alcohol epitomizes the "wretch saved by grace," and therefore, the hope of the Church. If "redeeming love is [indeed their] theme" (W. Cowper), Christians might begin to give the flourishing world of recovery more attention. It sometimes seems as though God cut out a substantial portion of His heart in the late 1930s and hid it in church basements and community centers across the country and the world. There, in every AA meeting, it continues to beat loudly and healthily – despite the buckets of bad coffee and parking lots full of cigarettes.

Some Christians worry that Twelve Step programs do not use the word 'Jesus' very often. AA is quick to say that it is not a church. On a very basic level, complaining that AA does not talk enough Jesus is like complaining that churches do not spend enough time teaching computer science. Or, perhaps better, like critiquing Habitat for Humanity for spending too much time building houses and not enough in worship.

Yet, as outlined above, in AA there is only talk about God as the rescuer of troubled people. This particular understanding of God's character as simultaneously intervening and unfailingly merciful not only is uniquely Christian, but also it finds its full realization in history in the person of Jesus of Nazareth.

Christians may also object to AA's somewhat vague notion of "spirituality." For the many alcoholics disillusioned by Christianity, however, the broadness of a "spiritual" life allows them an entryway into the Christian message that might not otherwise exist. Think of it in terms of a romantic analogy.

Perhaps, as a college student, you develop a crush on a girl that you see around campus without knowing her name. After a few run-ins, which leave you excited and preoccupied, you begin to date. Instead of giving you her real name, however, she gives you a nickname, explaining that her family is well-known and that her real name carries with it many associations, some of them negative. She wishes for your impressions not to be swayed by her reputation. Of course, as the relationship develops in intimacy, her true identity must eventually be divulged; that is simply part of knowing her more deeply. This analogy may be overly generous, but it helps explain why so many AAs become devout Christians. While Christianity, and religion more broadly, often carry negative associations, Alcoholics Anonymous allows many people an entryway into religion which may not otherwise exist. The two worlds of AA and Christianity, therefore, could learn from each other immensely.

Human Nature through the Lens of Addiction

"Those who are predisposed to fall into despondency as well as to rise into the ecstasy may be able to view reality from an angle different from that of ordinary folk. Yet it is a true angle; and when the problem or the religious object has been once so viewed, others less sensitive will be able to look from a new vantage point and testify that the insight is valid." [5]
-Roland Bainton

Bainton appears to be saying that one person's extremity may reveal an aspect of truth that applies to all people. Such is the case with addiction, which paints a portrait of the human condition in very stark brush strokes. As such, it offers considerably more insight than the picture we typically find in Hollywood, on the news, or in our own heads – where we all too often hear that we are free agents making choices, and that life is a matter of performance and accomplishment. Instead, addiction echoes the biblical portrait of original sin, where man is in conflict with God and unable to surrender his prerogatives.

To be clear, as far as the Twelve Steps are concerned, alcoholics are not free to choose sobriety. Bishop FitzSimons Allison once said, "The amazing thing about the alcoholic is that he can choose between gin and beer and whiskey, but he can't choose not to drink." This is the same view of humanity that we see played out in the Garden of Eden – that man is free to choose everything except the one thing he should be choosing: God, over and above himself. In traditional Protestant (or "Reformational") Christian doctrine, this idea is called the bound will. While the

---

[5] Roland Bainton, *Here I Stand: A Life Of Martin Luther* (New York: Signet Press, 1955), 283. Luther's psychological landscape, as Bainton portrays it, was fraught with the sort of extreme, in some ways manic tendencies that we sometimes see in alcoholics.

unfree human will finds painfully clear expression in alcoholism, Christianity would claim that the problem is universal.

Any kind of behavior that willpower has proven insufficient in controlling or curbing – workaholism, manic depression, compulsive exercise, obsessive parenting, or road rage, to name just a few – offers a relevant glimpse into the problem of life which both AA and Christianity seek to address. Regardless of whether society views these proclivities positively or negatively, worldly accomplishment can indicate neurotic preoccupation as much as dire failure can. Our failure to control many of our own habits and inclinations makes the problem of addiction one which is, in some sense, universal. In that sense, this book is for everyone.

Who's Zoomin' Who? (Aretha Franklin, 1985)

An important issue for Alcoholics Anonymous is the problem of agency: in other words, is the emphasis placed on the individual's initiative or on God's work upon the individual?

For starters, it should be understood that the "work-related" terminology of the Twelve Steps can just as easily be interpreted as a descriptive tool, rather than a prescriptive one. In other words, the working of the Twelve Steps is what happens *to* the person who finds God's grace, rather than something that precedes the attainment of grace. 'Grace' here simply refers to a wholly undeserved gift, one which provides an irresistible and radical reorientation of the recipient's life. The movement of grace often happens with our consent, but it never happens on our initiative. Perhaps an analogy will help to make the point:

Imagine that you are riding on the deck of a cruise liner in the middle of the night. Suddenly, you slip on the slick flooring and find yourself tumbling overboard, into the cold dark waters below. You begin to flail in the choppy sea, kicking and trying to scream for help. Unfortunately, you're a poor swimmer and can barely keep your head above water, much less get your voice to project enough to be heard by the passengers and crew still on board. Miraculously, one of your shipmates spots you and yells to the captain, "Man overboard!" The crew makes the proper adjustments, and after not too long the ship pulls within reach of you. A life preserver ring attached to a rope is thrown from the deck, and it mercifully lands in front of you, just as your strength is failing.

You grab onto it with both arms, finding immediate relief in its buoyancy. The crew then draws the line into the boat and hoist you onto the deck where you lie, coughing the water out of your lungs, completely exhausted, befuddled, and grateful. The passengers and crew wrap you in blankets and carry you to the infirmary.

Imagine now that you finally have gotten your voice back. You motion that you wish to make a brief announcement to the onlookers. Here is what you say:

> *"Did you see how I grabbed onto that life preserver like an expert? Did you notice the strength of my biceps and the dexterity in my wrists? I was all over that thing!"*

Would not the people hearing this think you had lost your mind? Your statement misses the entire thrust of what had just occurred, which was – pure and simple – a rescue.[6] Would not gratitude and humility be a more fitting and natural response to the whole situation?

---

[6] The theological study of God as the rescuer of people is known as "soteriology." It is fair to say that AA's understanding of the spiritual life is unavoidably soteriological in its angling.

And yet, sadly enough, some form of the above tends to be our response to most of the good things that happen to us. Winners of poker games always believe they won by skill; losers tend to believe they were the victim of bad luck. Our careers, our children, our relationships: the human race has an incredible talent for focusing on its own role in the good things of life and minimizing its culpability in negative things. Religious people are not exempt from this phenomenon. In my experience, while Christians often talk loudly about God's power and grace, their rhetoric just as often betrays a secret belief that their own initiative and willpower played the decisive role – *"did you see the way I grabbed onto that life preserver?"*

In Alcoholics Anonymous, we have been disabused of our romance with our own willpower. The manner in which it failed us was dramatic, poignant, and explicit. As much as the Twelve Steps ostensibly emphasize action, the entire process is conditioned by profound dependence upon grace. Most alcoholics end up in AA after years of trying to cure themselves with self-help – indeed, self-help's failure is a starting-point for AA. In this sense, it is desperation and not virtue that fuels one's engagement with the AA Program. The step-'work' happens reflexively in the one who knows his need for rescue. To the extent that we honestly recognize our powerlessness to rescue ourselves, the message of grace breaks through by assuring us that we don't *have* to save ourselves. Indeed, this idea permeates all Twelve Steps of AA.

It is hard to imagine the drowning man rejecting the life preserver unless he were in some way deluded about the severity of his situation. Yet in the world of AA we find many such people – people who know themselves to be drowning in alcoholism and yet, somehow, still believe they can effect sobriety by exerting their willpower more effectively. These people rarely stay sober for long, but they often return years later with an entirely different understanding of their problem. This is why "powerlessness" is so heavily emphasized as the beginning of a sober life. Indeed, it is where Step 1 begins.

The Twelve Steps

1. We admitted we were powerless over alcohol—that our lives had become unmanageable.

2. Came to believe that a Power greater than ourselves could restore us to sanity.

3. Made a decision to turn our will and our lives over to the care of God as we understood Him.

4. Made a searching and fearless moral inventory of ourselves.

5. Admitted to God, to ourselves, and to another human being the exact nature of our wrongs.

6. Were entirely ready to have God remove all these defects of character.

7. Humbly asked Him to remove our shortcomings.

8. Made a list of all persons we had harmed, and became willing to make amends to them all.

9. Made direct amends to such people wherever possible, except when to do so would injure them or others.

10. Continued to take personal inventory and when we were wrong promptly admitted it.

11. Sought through prayer and meditation to improve our conscious contact with God as we understood Him, praying only for knowledge of His will for us and the power to carry that out.

12. Having had a spiritual awakening as the result of these steps, we tried to carry this message to others, and to practice these principles in all our affairs.

I: SHAVING THE ENEMY

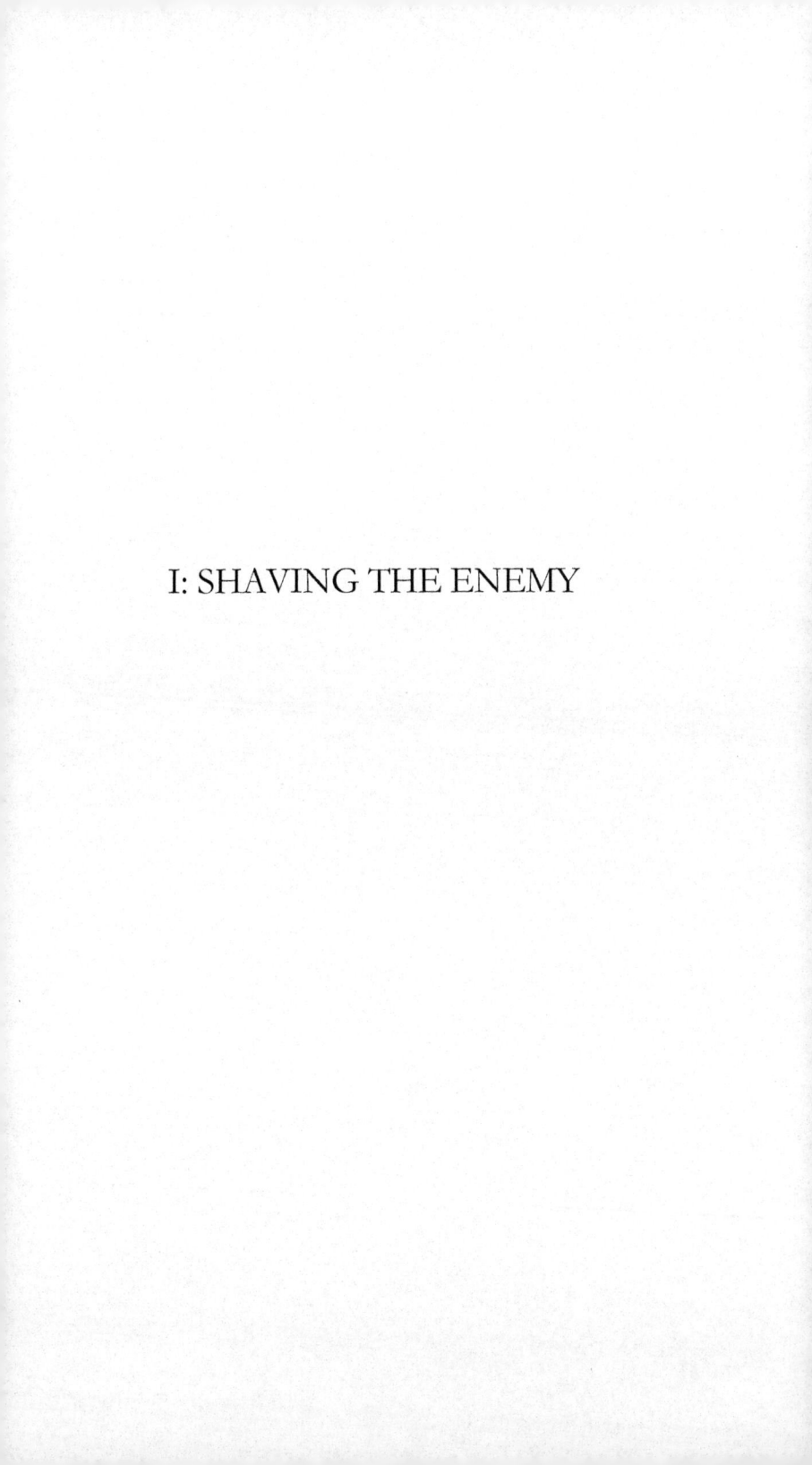

Step 1

"We Admitted We Were Powerless...That Our Lives Had Become Unmanageable."

"A death blow is a life blow to some,
Who 'til they died did not alive become.
Who had they lived had died.
But when they died vitality begun."
-Emily Dickinson, Poem 816

Do you remember the 1980s classic film *Sixteen Candles?* It tells the story of Claire's life on the day of her sixteenth birthday, which also happens to be the day of her older sister's wedding. Poor Claire quickly realizes that her family has completely forgotten about her birthday. No gifts await her; no one tells her "Happy birthday." And so the worst day of her life begins.

As the movie unfolds, her self-pity transforms from anger to apathy, and finally from apathy into despair. Despite this downward spiral, the viewer soon realizes that a second, more important plot is afoot. It involves Jake, the young man she has a crush on. She doesn't think that he even knows of her existence, but Claire is luckily mistaken – he knows exactly who she is. By the end of the film, through an amazing series of tragic and hilarious events, she finds herself celebrating her sixteenth birthday alone with Jake. When she finally blows out the candles on her cake, she doesn't have to make a wish because her wish has come true—it is sitting across from her! The worst day of her life has become the best.

The first of the Twelve Steps follows a similar pattern. It draws attention to the darkest aspects of life and, in so doing, opens the door to a second, unexpected narrative that is full of hope and promise.

One more movie illustration before we move on. Japanese director Akira Kurosawa made a film in 1952 called *Ikiru*. It begins with the ominous image of an X-ray of a man's stomach. There is a noticeable irregularity against the lower wall of the stomach's lining, which the voiceover narrator acknowledges as he introduces the plot: "here we see our protagonist's stomach. As you can tell from that tumor, he is very sick...*But he will have to get a lot worse before he can get better.*" The film's opening offers a perfect description of the dynamic that is at play in the 1st Step of the AA program.

As bad as things may be looking for the alcoholic who unexpectedly finds himself in an AA meeting one day, the reality is that whatever his particular set of troubles, they are probably only the tip of the iceberg. Whatever the presenting symptoms of "a life unmanageable" may be, they almost always point back in upon themselves to a deeper cancer at the root of our being, a cancer that must be exposed and confronted before there can be any talk of the symptoms improving. The fact that spiritual and personal awakenings must begin on such a depressing note might seem unfortunate, but if we had a more upbeat alternative to suggest, then we would offer it now. After all, it is only when the more attractive options have failed us that we become open to the kind of help that the Twelve Steps offer. They are the makeover that nobody wants to admit they need, but who wouldn't benefit from a makeover?

The Theology of AA: God Meets People at Their Point of Need

"Who cares to admit complete defeat? Practically no one, of course. Every natural instinct cries out against the idea of personal powerlessness."
-12 & 12 (21)

Right off the bat, it should be noted that *the spiritual experience offered in AA does not begin with talk of God.* One does not have to affirm any kind of faith, or even believe anything at all. The entire focus at the beginning of the Twelve Step approach centers upon the state of the individual. In other words, AA's theology is existential. It starts at the bottom, with the self and the facts on the ground, and only then does it look upward.

Of course, no one likes to look at themselves from the angle of failure or limitation. In fact, we often go to extremes to avoid doing so. I was employed for a time as a counselor at the New York City Rescue Mission, the city's oldest men's shelter. My job was to counsel men who had recently come off of the streets and to handle their intake into a nine-month Twelve Step rehabilitative program, which was designed to help them get back on their feet after long stints of homelessness and substance abuse. I met with every new man that came into the program for a year, and it was my job to ask each of them a certain series of questions. The answers were always the same:

John: "Hi, I'm John, how are you doing?"

Everyman: "I'm doin' great! I'm glad to finally be off the streets and getting my life in order. I want to make something of my life, and I know that it's time. Thanks be to Jesus!"

John: "What brings you here to our program?"

Everyman: "Well, I had some tough times. I got messed up... but we don't need to talk about that any more, now that I'm here. Thanks be to Jesus!"

John: "I hope you don't mind, but I need to ask you a few more specific questions about your history. Were drugs or alcohol big factors in your life before you got here?"

Everyman: "Well, yes, I got a little messed up with drugs and alcohol...but I'm done with that now, thanks be to Jesus!

John: "Did you say that you used to smoke crack?"

Everyman: "Yeah, you know, I messed around with that stuff some...Jesus, Jesus, JESUS!"

In every instance, the newcomer had a severe history with drug addiction, alcoholism, or mental illness, always to the point where his addiction had taken precedence over all other aspects of his life. After a period of homelessness while he pursued his addiction headlong, he would eventually arrive at the shelter in a devastated state. When asked about their hardships, however, not one of them was forthright in sharing their struggles. Instead, they attempted to hide or divert attention from the seriousness of their situation, often employing spiritual lingo to do so.[7]

The inability to look sin in the eye is active, even to the broken man who has lost everything but his own life! This dilemma was perfectly summarized by FitzSimons Allison in 1962: "A lot of nonsense is talked about our seeking after God, when actually the exact opposite is the case."[8] Sure, we may want God's help – just not in the area where we actually need it. Like a dog in a veterinarian's office trying to avoid having a cast put on its broken leg, we struggle against the very thing we need to heal us.

The first of the Twelve Steps requires the "admission of powerlessness"; the addict cannot access sobriety without traveling through that ugly door. In a practical sense, this means that the addict who is not in a state of despair about her plight must be made to feel worse if she is to find lasting sobriety.[9]

Different Pictures of the Same Person

"The only difference between men and rats is that rats learn from their mistakes." -B. F. Skinner

Consider this recent headline from 2010: "Guy Shoots Himself While Sleepwalking." The reporter writes:

---

[7] A theological term for this mindset is "total depravity", or the idea that humans are both fundamentally sinful and unwilling to recognize their sinfulness. This idea was formulated by Augustine and emphasized by John Calvin during the Protestant Reformation.
[8] C. FitzSimons Allison, *Fear, Love, and Worship* (Vancouver, British Columbia: Regent College Publishing, 1962), 12.
[9] This need-based model finds its closest theological parallel in the world of traditional Lutheranism, where the sinner must be crushed by his inability to meet God's demand (Law) before he will turn to appreciate the Gospel.

> "Why do people keep loaded guns near their bed while they sleep? For every crime in progress this stops, another three or four guys probably shoot themselves while sleepwalking." *Like this man, who shot himself in the knee.* According to the Boulder Daily Camera, sixty-three year old Sanford Rothman woke up at around 2:00 a.m. to a loud 'Bang!' He'd shot himself in the knee with the nine-millimeter handgun he keeps by his bed. Rothman was treated at a local hospital and released."[10]

This is not a satirical article from *The Onion*—it is a real article about a real person—and we offer it as an amusing portrait of human nature as we have come to see it through the lens of the Twelve Steps. This somewhat darkly tinted view is not only espoused by AA, but also by the worlds of contemporary psychology and, intriguingly, traditional Christian theology.

A classic example of this position comes from the wonderful letter that St Paul wrote to the Galatian church. Paul writes: "For the sinful nature desires what is contrary to the spirit, and the spirit what is contrary to the sinful nature. They are in conflict with each other, so that *you do not do what you want*" (5:17).[11] The landscape described looks like a battlefield, full of ongoing conflict in which the bad tends to win out over the good, vaguely reminiscent of the Disney image of Donald Duck with an angel on one shoulder and a devil on the other.[12] Again, we think of Dynasty: "I Don't Wanna Be a Freak (But I Can't Help Myself)."

In reflecting on ourselves, we can see two people in the same shell: there is the person we aspire to become, and then there is the person who watches too much television, the one who never

---

[10] Adrian Chen, "Guy Shoots Himself While Sleepwalking", *Gawker*, October 27, 2010, http://www.gawker.com/.

[11] Except where otherwise noted, emphasis in quotes is added by the author.

[12] It is worth noting that the devil beats the angel in every one of these classic cartoon debates.

makes use of the gym membership. These two people live discordantly in the same body, and their tense interplay tells much of the story of what it means to be human. William Faulkner had the same insight when, in his Nobel Prize speech, he claimed that all good literature concerns "the human heart in conflict with itself."

Understanding life's dilemmas in this way is crucial if the problem of alcoholism is to be properly addressed. The Big Book, which is the basic text of Alcoholics Anonymous, makes the same point with a classic illustration about a jaywalker:

> "Our behavior is as absurd and incomprehensible with respect to the first drink as that of an individual with a passion, say, for jaywalking. He gets a thrill out of skipping in front of fast-moving vehicles. He enjoys himself for a few years in spite of friendly warnings. Up to this point you would label him as a foolish chap having queer ideas of fun. Luck then deserts him and he is slightly injured several times in succession. You would expect him, if he were normal, to cut it out. Presently he is hit again and this time has a fractured skull. Within a week after leaving the hospital a fast-moving trolley car breaks his arm. He tells you he has decided to stop jaywalking for good, but in a few weeks he breaks both legs.
>
> On through the years this conduct continues, accompanied by his continual promises to be careful or to keep off the streets altogether. Finally, he can no longer work, his wife gets a divorce and he is held up to ridicule. He tries every known means to get the jaywalking idea out of his head. He shuts himself up in an asylum, hoping to mend his ways. But the day he comes out he races in front of a fire engine, which

breaks his back. Such a man would be crazy, wouldn't he?

You may think our illustration is too ridiculous. But is it? We, who have been through the wringer, have to admit if we substituted alcoholism for jaywalking, the illustration would fit exactly. However intelligent we may have been in other respects, where alcohol has been involved, we have been strangely insane."[13]

Let us now turn to the account of human behavior found in the New Testament. The disciples who accompanied Jesus to the garden of Gethsemane exhibit undeniably jaywalker-like tendencies. In fact, the description of how Jesus' closest friends acted in the moments right before he was arrested and crucified is nothing short of devastating. The events take place after Jesus had finished three years of full-time ministry:

> "They went to a place called Gethsemane, and Jesus said to his disciples, 'Sit here while I pray.' He took Peter, James, and John along with him and he began to be deeply distressed and troubled.
>
> 'My soul is overwhelmed with sorrow to the point of death', he said to them. 'Stay here and keep watch.'
>
> Going a little farther, he fell to the ground and prayed that if possible the hour might pass from him.
>
> 'Abba, Father', he said, 'everything is possible for you. Take this cup from me. Yet not what I will, but what you will.'

---

[13] Bill Wilson and Robert Smith, *Alcoholics Anonymous* (New York, NY: Alcoholics Anonymous World Services Inc., 2001), 37-38.

> Then he returned to his disciples and found them sleeping.
>
> 'Simon', he said to Peter, 'are you asleep? Couldn't keep watch for one hour? Watch and pray, so that you will not fall into temptation. The spirit is willing, but the flesh is weak.'
>
> Once more he went away and prayed the same thing. When he came back, he *again found them sleeping*, because their eyes were heavy. They did not know what to say to him.
>
> Returning the third time, he said to them, 'Are you *still* sleeping and resting? Enough! The hour has come.'"[14]

What are we to say of Jesus' final impressions of human nature in the hours before he was taken away to be crucified? One wonders if, had just one disciple been awake upon his return, Jesus wouldn't have said, "Phew, I don't have to go through with this. There's hope for these folks yet." But that does not happen. Right up until the end, the people closest to Jesus did not seem to have the power to do anything other than disappoint him.

It is worth pointing out that here, in this classic bit of Lenten Scripture, we find two understandings of human nature. There is the inaccurate one held by the disciples about themselves, and then there is the one that is empirically true. Just as Peter had earlier promised he would never deny Jesus, here too the disciples think they are capable of obeying their Lord, of controlling their behavior, and of following through with their intentions. But they are not. That notion turns out to be what Socrates would call "a wind egg" – a useless notion, a nonstarter. Their romantic

---

[14] Mk 14:32-42. All Bible quotes are from the NIV translation. After the disciples had fallen asleep, Peter then fumbles a second time. After swearing his allegiance and loyalty, he denies Jesus three times in rapid succession.

impressions of themselves cannot account for their behavior. The text, however, accounts for it completely. It sees through human nature, and it understands the crucifixion as a direct response to the disciples' state of weakness and self-delusion.

The historical narrative remains identical, from the 1939 account of alcoholism all the way back to the report of what happened 2000 years ago in the Garden of Gethsemane.[15] Human beings are driven by their self-defeating chemistry; the narrative of wise decision-making does not bear out in reality. Like the paintings of Botero that caricature their subjects in obese proportions, we find an uncomfortable ugliness when we look below the surface of our lives.

Fortunately (or unfortunately), we do not have to look exclusively to the past to find ourselves described accurately – we may also look to the world of psychology. Sigmund Freud famously pitted the id against the superego in a way that perfectly maps onto the material being discussed. And recent years have witnessed a deluge of social psychology studies that draw similar conclusions from empirical data.[16] The following excerpt, for example, comes from an article written by David McRaney about the way people choose which movies to watch on Netflix:[17]

> "If you have Netflix, especially if you stream it to your TV, you tend to gradually accumulate a cache of hundreds of films you think you'll watch one day. This is a bigger deal than you think. Take a look at your

---

[15] For those interested in biblical criticism, the Bible's deliberate parallel between Genesis and Gethsemane makes this exact point: placed in ideal conditions, we will always replicate our Fall.
[16] See Daniel Wegner's *The Illusion of Conscious Will* or David Eagleman's *Incognito: The Secret Lives of the Brain*.
[17] For those who don't use Netflix, it's a subscription website that mails DVDs to its users each month or allows them to watch movies online. The queue is a personal list of films that the user plans to watch through Netflix.

queue. Why are there so many documentaries and dramatic epics collecting virtual dust in there?

...A study conducted in 1999 by Read, Loewenstein and Kalyanaraman had people pick three movies out of a selection of twenty-four. Some were lowbrow, like "Sleepless in Seattle" or "Mrs. Doubtfire." Some were highbrow, like "Schindler's List." In other words, it was a choice between movies which promised to fun and forgettable or would be memorable but would require more effort to absorb...Most people picked "Schindler's List" as one of their three. They knew it was a great movie because all their friends said it was. All of the reviews were glowing, and it earned dozens of the highest awards. Most didn't, however, choose to watch it on the first day... This is sometimes called "present bias", being unable to grasp that what you want will change over time. And what you want now isn't the same thing you will want later. Present bias explains why you buy lettuce and bananas only to throw them out later when you forget to eat them.

Present bias is why you've made the same resolution ten years in a row but this time—you "mean it." You are going to lose weight and forge a six-pack of abs so ripped you could deflect arrows...One day, you have the choice between running around the block or watching a movie. You choose a movie. Another day you're out with friends and have a choice between a cheeseburger and a salad. You choose the cheeseburger. The slips become more frequent. But you keep saying you'll get around to it. You'll start again on Monday, which becomes a week from Monday. Your will succumbs to a death by a thousand cuts...

You can try to fight it back. You can buy a daily planner and a to-do list application for your phone. You

> can write yourself notes and fill out schedules. You can become a productivity junkie surrounded by instruments to make life more efficient, *but these tools alone will not help, because the problem is not that you are a bad manager of your time. You are a bad tactician in the war inside your brain.*"

Throughout all of history, from the prophets of Baal to the writings of Rousseau, from Thomas Jefferson to Oprah Winfrey, we have wanted something different to be true. But the story has not changed, nor will it. Indeed, until the guillotine-like reality is acknowledged with all of its attendant implications, little spiritual headway is ever made. *The realization of powerlessness that lies at the heart of the 1st Step comes to those who have lost confidence in themselves through a string of successive defeats.* It is the last stop on the bus.

Simply put, the Twelve Steps are not appealing at the outset. They are only ever completed by those who grasp their necessity. Step 1 hammers home the final nail in the coffin of our naïve hope in our own abilities.

Powerlessness: "Where do I start, where do I begin?" (The Chemical Brothers)

"The great and merciful surprise is that we come to God not by doing it right but by doing it wrong!"
-R. Rohr

A newcomer to AA spoke up in a meeting. She claimed that when she finally understood the 1st Step – the fact that she was an alcoholic – she "got a warm feeling all over. I finally knew that everything was going to be okay." A wise old-timer (someone who's been in the program a long time, often one with many years of sobriety) responded to her comment, saying in turn that "the only warm feeling I got when I understood the 1st Step came from the piss that was running down my leg." It's a rather crass way of making the point, but it affirms that the initial truth of the 1st Step is bad news, not good news. In and of itself, the 1st Step offers no encouragement. In fact, it discourages. It pulls the rug out from under us, and an appropriate response to this personal checkmate is fear. The 1st Step is the recognition that our faculties are insufficient to surmount the internal and external obstacles that we encounter in a fallen world.

In spite of how human wiring for self-preservation stands in unending opposition to weakness, the first of the Twelve Steps requires the "admission of powerlessness." As we mentioned earlier, sometimes the addict must be made to feel worse before recovery can begin. I remember the story of a wise AA named Chuck T., who was asked to visit the penthouse apartment of a man who had called an AA hotline. Chuck drove to a high-rise apartment building on the fancier side of Cleveland, an area called "the Gold Coast" with which he was not at all familiar. He took the elevator to the top floor. When the door opened, Chuck stepped into plush shag carpeting that came up to his ankles. The whole apartment was lined with windows, and he couldn't help but notice the incredible view of the entire city at night. He walked into the living room, where he found an ill-tempered man sitting on a white leather couch, with a martini glass in his hand.

Chuck introduced himself: "I'm here from AA." The man looked Chuck up and down and said, "I want to kill myself."

"Do you have a pen and paper handy?" asked Chuck in response.

"Didn't you hear me? I want to kill myself!"

Chuck answered, "Yes, I heard you. Did you hear me? I need a pen and a piece of paper." The agitated fellow pointed back toward the kitchen and muttered something. Chuck left the room, he returned a few moments later with a pen and paper in hand.

Chuck placed them on the coffee table in front of the guy, and then he said,

"If you sign all of this over to me, I'll push you." The man was completely undone by this unanticipated suggestion. It opened the door to a very important conversation. And so another member of AA began his walk into sobriety.

This tale illustrates the great spiritual insight that lies on the front end of AA's understanding of spiritual growth — that it begins with defeat. Chuck's offer to push the man drove him in the direction of apparent hopelessness, but it was precisely there that the man found counterintuitive hope and the beginnings of recovery. The brilliant insight at the core of AA's theology is this: *a person finds real hope by being directed away from false hope.*

The idea itself is not foreign to traditional Christian thought. The nineteenth-century Christian thinker Søren Kierkegaard was fond of trying to inspire the same kind of reaction in his readers. Attempting to make a similar point, he once wrote an essay entitled "Thoughts That Wound from Behind — for Upbuilding." He also famously described the sometimes-constructive roles of despair and anxiety in Christian life. Along the same lines, in his book *Grace in Practice*, Paul Zahl points out that "theology does not start from the top; it begins from the bottom…It begins with our enmeshed and constricted need."[18] It is doubtful that Chuck T ever read any of these pieces, but these same truths of human life have been observed and articulated by many different people.

By emphasizing weakness in Step 1, AA is actually teaching us something theological: The Twelve Steps posit that God is found primarily in the midst of weakness — not in strength. He

---

[18] Paul F.M. Zahl, *Grace in Practice: A Theology of Everyday Life* (Grand Rapids, MI: Eerdmans, 2007), 94.

saves people primarily from themselves. In this respect, He is rightly understood to be a "savior." Of course, rescue is also the thrust of the Bible's message and the heart of the Christian Gospel.

It is unfortunate that this simple catch-22 – that the only way you can find God is if you desperately need Him – stands in direct opposition to the widespread, even dominant notion in today's churches that the spiritual life begins with bold decision and virtuous intention, usually a personal choice to believe in God or to live a morally sound lifestyle. People in contemporary churches occasionally talk of God as redeemer, but there is also an enormous amount of rhetoric about God as teacher, friend, inspiration, or coach. In AA, there is only one thing: *God is who you need to save you.* And if you do not find Him, you are in serious trouble – in exactly the way the jaywalking example illustrates.

Gerhard Forde modeled his understanding of spirituality on the same view of human nature which AA affirms. Using the realities of addiction as a tool for understanding our spiritual predicament, he writes:

> "I use the analogy of addiction throughout the book in the attempt to demonstrate the difference between the theologian of glory and the theologian of the cross. The theologian of glory is like one who considers curing addiction by optimistic exhortation. The theologian of the cross knows that the cure is much more drastic... [Theologians of the cross] operate on the assumption that there must be – to use the language of treatment for addicts – a 'bottoming out' or an 'intervention.'
>
> That is to say, *there is no cure for the addict on his own.* In theological terms, we must come to confess that we are addicted to sin, addicted to self, whatever form that may take, pious or impious...'The remedy for curing

desire does not lie in satisfying it, but in extinguishing it.' The cross does the extinguishing. The cross is the death of sin, and the sinner. The cross does the 'bottoming out.' The cross is the 'intervention'...*'For a resurrection to happen, there must first be a death.'* The truth must be heard and confessed; then there is hope. A new life can begin, and with it a new sense of self-worth can blossom. For in the end we arrive, as we shall see, at the love of God, which creates anew out of nothing. So we begin the journey."[19]

If Forde is right, then AA possesses a profound understanding of some of the deeper and more elusive spiritual ideas that lie at the heart of the Christian faith. For the spiritually hungry AA member looking to explore more deeply the gut-level material he has encountered in the program, church history will provide a rich harvest.

At the same time, contemporary churches aren't always entirely faithful to the Christian tradition – especially in their view of human nature. AA, therefore, can help the Church recover parts of its own history. The spiritual dynamics of the 1st Step could be a welcome influence in mainstream evangelical culture. Imagine, for example, that you're walking into a church. To be admitted through the front door, you're forced to sign a waiver that says, "I'm a sinner and by stepping into the room today I acknowledge that fact." Though it would probably make you uncomfortable and nervous at the door, it would ultimately be comforting, and it would communicate an honest view of ourselves and others, one that might dispel the feelings of pressure

---

[19] Gerhard O. Forde, *On Being a Theologian of the Cross: Reflections on Luther's Heidelberg Disputation, 1518* (Grand Rapids, MI: Eerdmans, 1997), 15-17, 19.

and moral judgment which have repelled many from the church's doors.

Of course, you can come into church these days and sign up for any number of identities: casual Christmas and Easter churchgoer, devout and "good" Christian, intellectual believer with all the right answers – the list goes on, but the simple (and, incidentally, biblical) label of "sinner" is not one we usually wish to assume. This church environment often disillusions church regulars, repels potential members, and can cripple people's ability to be honest about their shortcomings. To be just a sinner, plain and simple, is often foreign to the practical, daily culture of churches, even though this identity is the foundational one in classic Christianity.[20]

In AA, on the other hand, there is only the option of sinner. It is sometimes said in AA that "a person doesn't attend AA in order to stay sober; they attend in order to remember that they are drunks." In this sense, AA's view of human nature and its corresponding view of sanctification are closely intertwined. We see this clearly in the Twelve Steps' repeated theme that a person changes by considering one's reluctance to change. When God allows an individual to see the (ugly) truth about human nature and agency, genuine transformation naturally follows. When God allows a group to see these truths, an environment of compassion, honesty, and openness prevails.

These ideas aren't foreign to Christianity; indeed, they're derived from it. In three of the four Gospel accounts, for example, Jesus plainly addresses the concern of inwardness: "Nothing that enters a person from the outside can defile him…what comes out of a

---

[20] In 1 Timothy, Paul writes that "Christ Jesus came into the world to save sinners – of whom I am the worst" (1:15). His own identity of "sinner" is fundamental for Paul's understanding of Jesus as rescuer.

person is what defiles him" (Mk 7:18-20) External conduct does little to help someone; Jesus compares the most outwardly respectable people to "whitewashed tombs" (Mt 23:27). Like Jesus, AA approaches external problems by dealing first with the internal issues. These issues must be addressed through a death to one's illusion of self-reliance, so that "whoever loses their life for me will save it" (Lk 9:24). This backhanded movement of recovery defines AA. Again, this knowledge of our own limitations and its attendant humility prepares the way for true spirituality: "It is not the healthy who need a doctor, but the sick. [Jesus did not] come to call the righteous, but sinners" (Mk 2:17). And so Step 1 expresses, in a beautiful way, a fundamental point of Christian doctrine.

For both the Church and for AA newcomers, this idea of our own limitations is unattractive. AA's ingredients of desperation and disillusionment with willpower force alcoholics to acknowledge the truth that they are sick, limited, internally sinful. And yet it's still a hard truth to sell. A Franciscan monk named Richard Rohr voiced the frustration inherent in sharing this sobering viewpoint with others:

> "How do you make attractive that which is not? How do you sell nonsuccess? How do you talk descent when everything is about ascent? How do you talk about dying to a church trying to appear perfect?... This is not going to work (which might be my first step)."[21]

So how does this theological bent apply directly to the life of the non-alcoholic individual?

---

[21] Richard Rohr, *Everything Belongs: The Gift of Contemplative Prayer* (New York, NY: Crossroad Publishing, 2003), 26.

Step 1 for Everyone: Life Unmanageable

"Everyone either has a problem, is a problem, or lives with a problem."
-Sam Shoemaker

One might ask where the non-alcoholic is to find a foothold in the 1st Step without taking up a rather rigorous program of drinking and substance abuse. This dilemma has been present in AA ever since its inception: it was first thought that only severe alcoholics were able to gain access to the program of recovery because of the "bottoming out" required to motivate someone to work the Twelve Steps. The necessary ingredient was described as "the gift of desperation."

Needless to say, AAs soon discovered that a bottom could be raised to the point where it would hit a potential alcoholic as long as the evidence of a problem was already manifesting itself. A person did not have to hit the low depths that many had reached in order to begin recovery. She only had to come to view the symptoms of her problem in relation to the same underlying problems suffered by alcoholics: addiction, powerlessness, defeat, unmanageability, or limitation.[22]

We can say with great confidence that the only person lacking desperation is the one who does not know herself very well. Usually a few examples of typical, universal human difficulty are enough to "raise the bottom" to the point where the idea of powerlessness will connect with any layperson. Let's explore some of these.

---

[22] "It was obviously necessary to raise the bottom the rest of us had hit to the point where it would hit them. By going back in our own drinking histories, we could show that years before we realized it we were out of control, that our drinking even then was no mere habit, that it was indeed the beginning of a fatal progression" (*12 & 12*, 23).

Commonplace Powerlessness in the Non-Alcoholic

"Left to my own devices (I probably would)" -Pet Shop Boys

Every person lives a life rife with powerlessness. Whether or not they are reticent to face their own weaknesses in no way determines whether or not they have them. Søren Kierkegaard posited as much in his book *Sickness unto Death* when he wrote:

> *"It makes no difference whether the person in despair is ignorant that his condition is despair — he is in despair just the same*...Compared with the person who is conscious of his despair, the despairing individual who is ignorant of his despair is simply a negativity further away from the truth and deliverance...This form of despair (ignorance of it) is the most common in the world."[23]

Step 1 allows individuals to reflect upon the "unmanageable" aspects of their lives, developing the sort of honesty which Kierkegaard espoused.

Like Swiss cheese, people are full of holes. The Twelve Step approach is quick to draw attention to those holes, rather than try to dodge, cover, or counterbalance them. So which weaknesses tend to be present universally? The Big Book provides its own list:

> "We had to ask ourselves why we shouldn't apply to our human problems this same readiness to change our point of view. We were having trouble with personal relationships, we couldn't control our emotional natures, we were prey to misery and depression, we couldn't make a living, we had a feeling of uselessness, we were

---

[23] Søren Kierkegaard, *The Sickness unto Death*, trans. Howard V. Hong and Edna H. Hong (Princeton, NJ: Princeton UP, 1980), 44-45.

full of fear, we were unhappy, we couldn't seem to be of real help to other people…" (52)

I have yet to meet the person who cannot identify with a least one of the items on that list. Who, for example, is a stranger to fear? Jesus offered a similar list in his famous Sermon on the Mount, but his list also included anger, lust, and anxiety. These are the "classics", and they account for much of the content of the day-to-day experience of being human.[24]

Using similar logic, AA would liken sin to sickness. R. C. Sproul voiced this sentiment when he wrote, "We are not sinners because we sin; we sin because we are sinners." We would happily extrapolate along those same lines: "we are not alcoholics because we drink uncontrollably; we drink uncontrollably because we are alcoholics." Have you ever thought of misdoing as a kind of illness? Like an allergy or a virus, self-centeredness cannot easily be mastered or controlled. The good news is that our negative attributes can become a bedrock upon which effective spirituality can be built. Without them, there is no hope for spiritual rejuvenation; in the place of health, there is apparently no need for recovery.

The realization of our own weakness is so counterintuitive to human nature that the revelation can be rightly ascribed to the divine. A Christian would ascribe this work to the Holy Spirit. The old-fashioned word for it is repentance.[25]

---

[24] At this point in the reading, you might pause for five minutes, and ask yourself: where is my life unmanageable? What things am I afraid of (even though I know better)? Am I angry at anyone? What makes me angry? What makes me anxious? What are my worst personality traits according to others? Do they have a point? Do I have any tendencies that tend to get in the way of my relationships with other people? In what ways, if any, do I try to justify these traits and tendencies? What are my worst problems in life?

[25] Along similar lines, a passage from Scripture comes to mind. "Godly sorrow brings repentance that leads to salvation and leaves no regret…" (2 Cor 7:10).

And so it is with the entire progression of AA's Twelve Steps. As the ego is deflated and self-confidence is discouraged at every turn, something called "faith", or "God-confidence" miraculously begins to take its place – although it doesn't appear that way to the subject at first. In Step 12, AA refers to the fruit of this faith as "a spiritual awakening."

We close this section on Step 1 with an incisive quote from the sixteenth-century English theologian Richard Hooker:

> "*My eager protestations, made in the glory of my ghostly strength, I am ashamed of; but those crystal tears, wherewith my sin and weakness was bewailed, have procured my endless joy; my strength hath been my ruin, and my fall my stay.*"

Step 2

"Came to Believe That a Power Greater Than Ourselves Could Restore Us to Sanity."

"Of course we must believe; but only because there is nothing left for us to do but believe."
-Robert Farrar Capon

"First you 'come.' Then you 'come to.' Then you 'come to believe.'"
-AA slogan

Have you heard the one about the broke farmer? He decided that he would have to sell his prize female pigs in order to keep his business afloat. So he loaded his pigs into the back of his truck and headed to the State Fair. When he got there, he met another farmer who was in a very similar position, only he was in possession of a bunch of prize male pigs. And so the two of them hatched a plan: rather than selling their pigs, they would mate them and sell off the piglets.

The only problem was finding a place where the pigs could mate, as their farms were sixty miles apart. After some discussion, they decided to meet at a field about thirty miles from each of their farms.

The next morning, the farmer drove his pigs to the rendezvous point and sent them off into the field to mate with the males. While they waited together, he asked his new buddy, "How will I know when they're pregnant?" The farmer replied, "The easiest way is this: when you get up in the morning, if your pigs are out grazing in the meadow, then they're pregnant. If your pigs are playing around in the mud, then they're not pregnant."

So the next morning the farmer woke up early and ran to the window to watch his pigs. They were all in the mud, so he hosed them off, loaded them into the back of the truck, and drove to the meeting point. The next morning he woke up, and again he found the same thing: the pigs were not in the field but in the mud. So each day he continued to drive them to meet the males.

Things continued this way for a few exhausting weeks, until one morning he slept through his alarm. His wife came upstairs to wake him.

He said, "Oh, I overslept. Will you just do me a quick favor and look out the window to see if the pigs are in the mud or in the field?"

She walked over and looked out the window.

"Neither", she said. "They're in the back of the truck and one of them is in the front, honking the horn."

It's a silly story, but it points to the idea that oftentimes there is a difference between what we think has been happening and what has actually been happening. The early portion of the Twelve Steps understands this. The first few steps offer a person the opportunity to look back over his life and recent events. What he often finds is that there are different ways to make sense of his past, and his prior explanations are not always sufficient to explain his self-destructive behavior.

Step 2 advocates that people "come to believe in a power greater than themselves." In the last chapter, we spoke at some length about the backhanded movement of the AA method, that the Twelve Steps bring a person to where they need to be by drawing attention not to the ideal, but rather to the individual's distance from that ideal. Step 2 continues in this vein, beginning with a reflection on one's own reluctance towards belief.

Hairballs and Personal Religious History

"The light shines in the darkness, and the darkness has not overcome it."
-John 3:5

A few years ago a movie called *Junebug* was released. It tells the story of a worldly, sophisticated New Yorker who falls in love with and marries a successful art dealer. He is originally from rural North Carolina and slightly embarrassed about his humble roots. Nonetheless, when business brings them to the vicinity, he decides to introduce his new bride to his family. During the visit, they find themselves attending a pancake supper at the church he grew up in, where he used to sing in the choir. The pastor twists his arm into singing once again for the congregation. It's a moving scene, and we see that his new wife finds the moment quite stirring. The lead is reengaging with a side of his past that he's spent a lot of time trying to bury. This reengagement is an accurate portrait of many people's experience with Step 2.

Many of us only become willing to believe in something new after we have first realized our hesitation to do so. As a parallel, people tend to become more open-minded only after they have examined their closed-mindedness. Step 2 seeks to trigger spiritual growth with a similar approach.

An AA old-timer once observed that "Step 2 is all about defiance." People who need to change must become aware of the ways in which they are opposed to changing or have failed to do so. When it comes to spiritual conviction, people often have a block of bad memories, experiences, or justifications for their old way of life, much like hairballs in a cat's throat. If the hairball becomes too large, it cannot be digested and must instead be coughed up before new food can be consumed. Step 2 begins this process of coughing up one's past through personal reflection.

The primary author of the Big Book and cofounder of AA, Bill Wilson, relayed his equivalent of coughing up a hairball in a portion of the text entitled "Bill's Story". Apparently Bill was just starting to think about religious ideas afresh when a former drinking buddy appeared on his doorstep, sober and having "got religion" (9). As Bill spoke with his friend, he found himself thinking about the old ideas, impressions, and memories he had carried with him for so many years. We'll let him speak for himself:

> "[My friend] had come to pass his experience along to me – if I cared to have it. I was shocked, but interested. *Certainly I was interested. I had to be, for I was hopeless.*
>
> ...I had always believed in a Power greater than myself. I had often pondered these things... But that was as far as I had gone.
>
> With ministers, and the world's religions, I parted right there. When they talked of a God personal to me, who was love, superhuman strength and direction, I became irritated and my mind snapped shut against such a theory.

But my friend sat before me, and he made the point-blank declaration that God had done for him what he could not do for himself. His human will had failed. Doctors pronounced him incurable. Society was about to lock him up. Like myself, he had admitted complete defeat. Then he had, in effect, been raised from the dead, suddenly taken from the scrap heap to a level of life better than the best he had ever known!

Had this power originated in him? Obviously it had not. There had been no more power in him than there was in me at that minute; and this was none at all…

Despite the living example of my friend there remained in me the vestiges of my old prejudice. The word God still aroused a certain antipathy. When the thought was expressed that there might be a God personal to me this feeling was intensified. I didn't like the idea. I could go for such conceptions as Creative Intelligence, Universal Mind or Spirit of Nature but I resisted the thought of a Czar of the Heavens, however loving His sway might be. I have since talked with scores of men who felt the same way." (9-12)

Most of us are just like Bill in this regard. We harbor a religious history, usually one which stands in the way of immediate spiritual progress. It is must be "coughed up" before any forward movement can occur.[26] The amazing thing is that no other seeking, apart from these types of reflections, seems to be required to begin spiritual growth. The subject re-engages with his past and reflects on the extent to which he's been reluctant to consider

---

[26] Practically, AAs often do this by talking over the material with another person, one who is not antagonistic toward such ideas.

anything new. Again, someone "comes to believe" by acknowledging the extent to which he has been unwilling to do so.

It is astonishing that nothing has to be done, that things simply have to be voiced—as they are—in order for new changes to begin. The individual does not have to come to God. Instead, people begin coughing up religious hairballs once they are forced to acknowledge their powerlessness in Step 1. Because the alcoholic cannot save himself, he must look outside himself by re-examining his religious history. Coming to believe, as the opening AA slogan expresses, is merely a product of the now-familiar mix of meetings, desperation, humility, and honesty about oneself. As this mix pushes someone toward spiritual self-examination, belief naturally develops. God, in other words, comes to us.

Working Step 2

When I was a boy, my mother used to make disparaging comments about bubblegum chewing, especially when it was audible. For her, the sound of people "smacking their gum" was just about the worst thing in the world, and needless to say, her little sermons on the issue permanently shaped my own view of bubblegum. In a similar light, sometimes our past experience colors the way we evaluate new things. The Big Book is quick to warn us about such biased assessments of the world:

> "Do not let any prejudice you may have against spiritual terms deter you from honestly asking yourself what they mean to you…we often found ourselves handicapped by obstinacy, sensitiveness, and unreasoning prejudice. Many of us have been so touchy that even casual reference to spiritual things made us bristle with

antagonism. This sort of thinking had to be abandoned." (47-48)

At this point, you might pause to reflect upon your personal history with spirituality and religion: On a scale of 1 to 10, how willing are you to explore new ideas about spirituality? Did you have any experience with religion when you were growing up? What do you remember of it? What do you think about religion in general? Do you have any "scripts" about religious people that you have recited on more than one occasion? Perhaps you've decided that religious people are phonies because "actions speaking louder than words." If you've known religious people who have mistreated you or others, then perhaps you believe, as one AA newcomer said, that "the proof with religious people is in the pudding...and I have yet to taste any good religious pudding." Have you had any negative experiences with Christians? What happened? What events have helped define your position on spiritual matters? Have you ever had any positive spiritual experiences? Again, what happened?

These kinds of questions can help us to be more objective in our consideration of spiritual matters. They enable a person to work Step 2.

Step 3

"Made a Decision to Turn Our Will and Our Lives Over to the Care of God As We Understood Him."

"If I could live my life over again I'd change every single thing I've ever done."
-Ray Davies, lead singer of The Kinks

"Every morning I wake up, look the enemy dead in the eye…and then I shave him."
-AA saying

The animated film *Finding Nemo* tells the story of a young fish named Nemo and his father.[27] At the beginning of the movie, we learn that when Nemo was just an infant, his mother was eaten by

---

[27] Many of these insights about *Finding Nemo* came from Nick Lannon's entry in Mockingbird's *The Gospel According to Pixar* (Charlottesville, VA: Mockingbird, 2010).

a shark. Nemo's father, Marlin, blames himself for his wife's death, believing that he abandoned her at that crucial moment. As a result, Marlin becomes incredibly over-protective, the aquatic version of a hovering "helicopter parent." So much so, in fact, that he refuses to let Nemo attend school, even though his son is of kindergarten age. Marlin cannot relinquish the reigns of his son's care to anyone for fear that something terrible will happen. Nemo naturally becomes frustrated by his father's paranoia and starts to rebel.

Soon, in spite of Marlin's best attempts to maintain control of his son's well-being, Nemo is caught in a fisherman's net and taken to live in an aquarium. A devastated Marlin becomes even more fearful and controlling, his neurosis driven by a deep love for his son. And so he sets out in search of Nemo, embarking on a journey which takes him into many unsettling and dangerous situations. At a crucial moment in the movie, Marlin and his light-hearted (and seemingly unintelligent) friend Dory are sucked into the mouth of a whale and trapped there.

After a few minutes, the water begins to drain into the whale's belly, leaving huge pockets of air in its wake. Dory tells Marlin, "It's okay, I speak whale… He says we should swim to the back of his throat." Paralyzed with fear, Marlin replies, "No way! Of course that's what he wants; he wants to eat us!" Dory urges him to reconsider and then swims to the back of the whale's mouth without him. Marlin desperately grabs onto one of the protruding taste buds on the whale's tongue so that he won't be swallowed. But soon the water line recedes, and Marlin is left grasping the taste bud, holding his breath because he is now out of the water.

To the world of AA, Marlin's actions represent the opposite of all spirituality. Marlin, in attempting to hold onto a sense of personal control and autonomy, only manages to hurt himself. *The exact actions that Marlin believes will save him are actually the things that will kill him.*

Eventually, Marlin can hold his breath no longer. He loses his grip and falls to the back of the dark whale mouth, where Dory is waiting for him. Suddenly there is a tremendous surge of water, and they are expelled through the creature's blowhole into freedom in the open sea. When he comes to himself, Marlin realizes that Dory was right about the whale, that his approach had only created anxiety and, finally, that the whale knew better than he did.

Moments later Marlin finds Nemo, who is thrilled to be reunited with his father. On top of that, Marlin is overjoyed about his second chance at fathering his son. This story provides us with a helpful vantage point for making sense of Step 3, where "we made a decision to turn our will and our life over to the care of God…"

AAs frequently claim that God and the alcoholic are at odds with each other. They talk about the alcoholic who "takes his will back." This inability to permanently acquiesce once and for all to the will of God keeps a sober alcoholic in a never-ending state of working the Twelve Steps. The premise here is that God's will typically stands in opposition to the inclination of the alcoholic's self-centered will.[28] The church historian Karl Holl describes how Martin Luther perfectly understood this spiritual dynamic: "For domestic life, [Luther] gave the advice sober people have always given: *in case of doubt choose what is contrary to your natural inclinations.*"[29] One wise AA member put it like this: "I never let go of anything

---

[28] This is not just the case for newcomers, but for old-timers too. "You never graduate from having to work the Twelve Steps."
[29] Karl Holl, *The Reconstruction of Morality*, ed. James Luther Adams and Walter F. Bense (Minneapolis, MN: Augsburg publishing House, 1979). Another great example comes from the TV show *Seinfeld*, in an episode where a perennially jobless and lonely George decides that the path to success is doing the opposite of everything he would normally do.

that didn't have claw marks on it." We are like Marlin fighting the current in the whale's mouth, or like Jacob in the Old Testament as he wrestled with God throughout the night.

In the life of faith, we undergo the painful experience of losing what we want in order to find what God would instead offer. We lose the old way of doing things to find a new way. The experience of losing *to* God is one that ultimately brings joy.[30] God is much more powerful (and sneakier) than any individual's ability to dodge Him. God can even trick us into wanting the thing He wants for us. This is the case both in the initial encounter and in the fresh re-encounter with God.

Step 3 also has a baptismal vibe. The person who takes Step 3 desires to discover a new version of life. She prays a prayer asking God to take over. In this way, Step 3 ends in the loss of an old, failed life, suggesting that at some point a new life will be found or, rather, it will find you. In Christian terms, this step involves the death of the "old self" in hopes that God will resurrect someone anew.[31] As the Big Book puts it, "We were reborn" (63).

How it Works: Janet Jackson and "Control"

"Let me give you a truth that can make all the difference in the world: almost everything you think about doing to make something better is wrong and will only make that something worse...Trying harder doesn't work."
-Steve Brown, *Three Free Sins*

---

[30] We think this is an accurate assessment, though maybe it's more accurate to say that AA's approach brings less agony than any other approach.
[31] Theologically, this is the death of the "Old Adam" – the man who's constantly obsessed with his own priorities and desire for mastery over his world.

STEP 3

Again, Step 3 calls for a confrontation with the "unspiritual" life and the motivations that drive it, and as such, it is the first time that the program explicitly highlights the overarching and indissoluble tension between God and the self. As we find in one of the Big Book's more infamous passages: "Selfishness and self-centeredness. That, we think, is the primary root of all our troubles. [We are] driven by a hundred forms of fear, self-delusion and self-seeking" (62). How do these factors play out in the human heart, and what is their role in perpetuating our doubts about God's better will for our lives?

In 1987, Janet Jackson released the hit single "Control." She sang, "Control, never gonna stop/ Control, to get what I want/ Control, got to have a lot." The song is a perfect encapsulation of the Marlin mentality. How many of us think that the key to individual success and happiness has to do with effort and internal volition? How many of us believe that willpower is the crucial factor in giving ourselves a life that is worth living? Popular advertising urges us to "never give up" or "just do it" or "make it happen", and pop culture constantly emphasizes "action" as the way forward. These slogans not only exist in our culture, but also they seem wired into the DNA of human existence – and this is a dire problem. The Big Book puts it like this:

> "Most people try to live by self-propulsion… Each person is like an actor who wants to run the whole show; is forever trying to arrange the lights, the ballet, the scenery and the rest of the players in his own way. If his arrangements would only stay put, if only people would do as he wished, the show would be great…What usually happens? The show doesn't come off very well…He decides to exert himself more" (61).

What is meant by "self-propulsion"? Propulsion is the forward drive or inertia of an object that determines its movement from one point to another. Think of a propeller. It spins, and the movement enables it to push whatever it is attached to forward. According to this analogy, the individual is trying to act as the driving force behind her own life. Self-propulsion is the idea that I am the one who makes myself move, or "I am the master of my fate: I am the captain of my soul", as the classic poem teaches students.[32]

One does not have to look far to find expressions of this philosophy. I recently saw a billboard in an airport which showed a young Indonesian girl, standing in the midst of a rice paddy. Next to her, in bold red letters, were the words: "I AM POWERFUL." The caption in no way described what I saw in the photograph. I saw two opposing ideas next to each other, yet separated by a vast gulf. There was assertion of power, inscribed in bold red letters. And then there was a child, a perfect portrait of all that is wonderful about the lack of power. I saw humility, weakness, beauty, and joy; lots of things, but not so-called "power."

People that "live by self-propulsion" understand themselves to be their own source of power. Their success hinges upon their performance. Step 3 questions the efficacy of this philosophy.[33]

In order to do so, the Big Book likens the addict to an actor "who wants to run the whole show; is forever trying to arrange the lights, the ballet, the scenery and the rest of the players in his own way." What is acting, and what does an actor do? Actors play the

---

[32] For what it's worth, these famous words from William Earnest Henley's "Invictus" were quoted by Timothy McVeigh, the Oklahoma bomber, as his final statement before his execution.

[33] The spiritual life espoused by AA typically identifies much more strongly with the child than with the slogan about power. Christianity, too, values the giving up of power far more than the assertion of it.

parts that are assigned to them. They assume the roles that are given to them. An actor prepares for his role by strict adherence to a script and occasional pointers from a director. But the actor we read about in the Big Book seems confused about his job description. If anything, he has very little interest in his own role, but an ambitious interest in the roles of the other players. What kind of acting is that? Bad acting at best.

There is a different name for the person who runs the show, who arranges the lights, the choreography, the scenery and the rest of the players. That person is called a "director." The Big Book metaphor describes *an actor who thinks he is a director*. Can you imagine the chaos that would break out on set if one of the actors tried suddenly to usurp the director's job? The chaos probably wouldn't last very long, because the actor would soon be on his way out the door and in search of a new job!

The actor who is trying to play the director is busy functioning in an incorrect capacity, and no amount of effort and good ideas on his part can change that. Similarly, charitable actions that are motivated by self-interest are misguidedly conceived, no matter how many warm smiles and polite gestures introduce them. They take little actual account of the other's well-being and, instead, view other people – even loved ones – as means to a personal end, which is usually an ill-conceived attempt at self-satisfaction and comfort. It is fair to say that our agendas often hamper our ability to be of service. In this respect, we see how love may quickly morph into manipulation.

In AA, people are understood to be actors, and "God is the director." This is not meant as an insult so much as a straightforward description of the natural order of creation. Imagine further the insanity that would ensue if *all* of the actors in a show somehow got the same wrong idea about their roles, and they *all* started trying to control the production simultaneously, each with a different idea of how the story should be written.

Would it not be like the argumentative first cousins who got into a pushing match when their grandmother arrived for a Thanksgiving visit? As the fight broke out, one of them screamed: "She's not your grandmother; she's mine!" Warring narratives make for bad friendships, and a bunch of confused actors is not a pleasant image. Do you know any confused actors?

Malcolm Gladwell commented on this problematic mindset in an interview about his book *Outliers: The Story of Success*. He was asked to what extent his book was actually an attack on the philosophy of "rugged individualism, and the myth of American success." His answer was illuminating:

> "In some ways this book is somewhere between a corrective and a full-scale assault on the way Western society in general and American society in particular has thought about success over the last few hundred years. You know, we have fallen in love with this notion of the self-made man, of the rags-to-riches story, of the idea that if you make it to the top of your profession you deserve a salary of 20 million dollars a year because you're the one responsible for getting to the top. Why shouldn't you be richly rewarded? And that idea and that ethos has permeated virtually every way in which we think about achievement, and I think that that idea is completely false; it's worse than false, it's dangerous!"

The respective worlds of AA and Christian theology both agree with Mr. Gladwell. The "self-made" idea is, at least if not "dangerous," still the very antithesis of spirituality. Of course, we might take it a step further, claiming that what Gladwell considers typical of "Western society in general and American society in particular" is in fact found in all cultures, though perhaps with varying sets of emphases. The idea of the self-made man is certainly far from unique, historically speaking.

A remarkably similar debate concerning spiritual self-propulsion occurred in the third century between a monk named Pelagius and a theologian named Augustine. Pelagius insisted that God had created people in such a way that their religious well-being was up to them. For him, everything centered on the attributes of self-discipline and unceasing effort. Though Pelagius admitted these traits were God-given, in practice his ideas allowed people to follow and defend their natural inclination toward being the masters of their souls. Augustine, like Gladwell, saw the fallacy of this reductionist and self-oriented train of thought. He knew that such a philosophy left little room for failure, and therefore no room for grace and the activity of God. The self-will approach was labeled a heresy by the early church, for it would have destroyed the need for the absolution upon which the Christian faith centered. Why would God, after all, create individuals in such a way that they would no longer have any need for Him?[34]

Step 3 does a wonderful job of separating the spiritual wheat from the well-intentioned but romantic chaff of the "self-made man". The Big Book puts it like this:

> "Above everything, we alcoholics must be rid of this selfishness. We must, or it kills us! God makes that possible. And there seems no way of getting rid of self without His aid. Many of us had moral and philosophical convictions galore but we could not live up to them, even though we would have liked to. Neither could we reduce our self-centeredness much by

---

[34] St. Paul himself took similar issue with a destructive group of theologians in Galatia in the First Century. He wrote: "I do not set aside the grace of God, for if righteousness could be gained through (obedience to) the law, Christ died for nothing!" (Gal 2:21).

wishing or trying on our own power. We had to have God's help...We could wish to be moral, we could wish to be philosophically comforted, in fact we could will these things with all our might, but the needed power wasn't there. *Our human resources, as marshaled by the will, were not sufficient; they failed utterly. Lack of power, that was our dilemma."* (62, 45)

As we saw in *Finding Nemo*, the philosophy of self-propulsion and self-direction fails in its attempt to create happiness. In fact, it often creates the exact opposite of the thing it intends: chaos and tragedy instead of peace and contentment. For this reason, AAs are fond of saying: "My best thinking got me here [to a state of destitution and alcoholism]."

Anything Would Be Better Than What I've Got

"...there was nothing left but to pick up the kit of spiritual tools that was laid at our feet..."
-*Big Book (25)*

At the very end of Whit Stillman's novelization of his film *The Last Days of Disco*, one of the lead characters, Des, sees the truth about himself for the first time:

> "Do you know the Shakespearean admonition 'To thine own self be true'?" [Des] asked.
> I nodded, of course.
> "It's premised," he said, "on the idea that 'thine own self' is something pretty good, 'being true' to which is 'commendable.' What if 'thine own self' is not so good? What if it's 'pretty bad'? Wouldn't it be better not

to be true to thine own self in that case? You see, that's my situation."[35]

Des hilariously expresses the 3rd Step insight, namely, that truth often feels more like a personal disintegration than a breakthrough. His remark is similar to what many in AA call a "spiritual ambush." Perhaps it's more like a surprise birthday party? Either way, the 3rd Step points to the idea that *God's work in the life of an individual is primarily and necessarily deconstructive.*

The world desperately needs an alternative to the philosophy of self-sufficiency, even if most of us are too belligerent to be aware of its existence. The good news we find in AA is that we do not need to be aware of better options in order to make spiritual progress. No understanding of the thing that lies on the other side of the veil is required. Exhaustion is the key. As one Church of England bishop put it, "God meets us at our point of need."

When self-defeating thought collapses in on itself, a newfound spirituality begins to seep in through the fissures. A fancy theological word for this is "apophaticism", or the method of arriving at truth through the process of deconstructing false ideas, rather than straightforwardly emphasizing true ones. In my own Damascus Road experience, I simply realized that I was living my life backwards.

True Mysticism: Life in Reality

"Reality is a great place to visit, but I wouldn't want to live there.
-AA Slogan

---

[35] Whit Stillman, *The Last Days of Disco, With Cocktails at Petrossian Afterwards* (New York, NY: Farrar Straus Giroux, 2000), 299.

If we are to live a spiritually fulfilling life, there are many misconceptions that will have to be dropped. Step 3 is the place where this occurs, as misguided people are called back to their senses. They are forced to reckon with reality, which usually involves a painful philosophical reorientation that results in a newfound humility.

Fear of the new is almost always the desire to avoid the loss of the old and familiar. Think of the sad sack young man who's just been dumped at the beginning of the 1996 movie *Swingers*. His buddies try to remind him that there are other fish in the sea. But he doesn't want another fish. Therein lies the rub. A famous passage in the *12 & 12* gives voice to this fear: "I'll look like the hole in the donut" (36). The truth is that when the ability to let go finally arrives, it will come from frustration and exhaustion rather than virtue. While this may sound pessimistic, it is not.

The primary obstacles to letting go are the now-familiar problems of selfishness and our delusions of grandeur. Being rid of these is deflating, but accepting the truth of our own limitations is in fact immensely life-giving and freeing. In child psychologist Dorothy Martyn's book, entitled *Beyond Deserving*, we read:

> "We adults do not like to face the fact that we are not the sole directors of our thoughts and actions, because it is a blow to our illusion of autonomy and power and pre-eminence in the universe…Given the more realistic understanding of the limitations of human autonomy, what does the word "responsibility" mean? In this light, responsibility changes its colors. We are more responsible, not less so, when we are aware of forces that are working on us beyond our ability to control them. Denial of that truth, along with actions that do

not take that truth into account, is the height of irresponsibility."[36]

In other words, this brand of Twelve Step spirituality enables a person to live within the midst of the fallen world, which is – simply put – reality.

The notion that God enables escape from problems is common in some forms of religious thinking. Martin Luther called such ideas "theologies of glory." Theologies of glory will be considerably more familiar to Christians than to those in AA. The idea more commonly held in AA is that God enables unmediated (i.e. sober) acceptance of problems, rather than the ability to sidestep them. Problems in no way indicate the absence of God—instead, they point the individual toward God. The same sentiment is rephrased nicely by the preacher T. D. Jakes: "God won't save you from the fire; He'll save you through the fire."

I experienced the truth of Step 3 firsthand early on in my ministry. I was sitting in my office one morning when I received a phone call. The woman on the other end of the line was in tears, telling me, "I've done something terrible! Can my husband and I come in to meet with you ...as soon as possible?" They were in my office an hour later, where she confessed to a recent affair. The husband looked completely dumbfounded, but he said he still loved her and wanted to try to salvage things.

Then he asked me something which put me in completely over my head: "We've been going through a tough time financially and, because of it, I've been reading my Bible a lot and praying more than usual. I really believe that God spoke to me recently. He told me: 'I am going to bless you.' What I want to know is...is *this* the blessing?" I didn't know how to respond, but I was eager to separate his thinking about God from the anguish he was

---

[36] Dorothy W. Martyn, *Beyond Deserving: Children, Parents, and Responsibility Revisited* (Grand Rapids, MI: Eerdmans, 2007),156.

experiencing in that moment. I asked him, "Does this feel like a blessing to you?" He glazed over; I had lost his ear. I couldn't connect. He seemed deep in thought and far away. It didn't take long for me to realize I was out of my depth and too inexperienced to properly counsel this couple.

Fortunately, one of my colleagues was a few rooms away and willing to help. I knew for a fact that he had counseled many couples back from the brink of divorce. I asked if we could meet with him to seek his wisdom and he immediately made himself available. A few minutes later, all four of us were sitting in his office.

The couple rehashed their situation, almost word for word. The wife was a wreck. The husband was numb and distant. After a lot of listening, my coworker asked the husband if there was anything he wanted to add to the story. The man repeated the same seemingly over-spiritualized statement about his devotional time and God's blessing. He asked, "Do you think that my wife's affair is God's blessing?"

Without missing a beat, my friend replied, "*Absolutely! This is the best thing that has ever happened to your marriage.* It has brought the two of you into reality and out of delusion. It is in that place that God is found, and it is in that place that you will find hope for your marriage." I thought to myself, *Whoa! There's no way that dog will hunt.* To my surprise, the man's posture completely changed. All at once he seemed to relax. He was finally able to cry. It was a powerful and deeply spiritual moment. Against my "better" judgment, my coworker had affirmed the man's twisted hunch, and the man suddenly felt hope. He felt understood. They continued to meet with this minister and are still married – and on more solid footing – to this day. It was a great lesson for me.

In this sense, living in reality is actually mystical. Martin Luther once asserted that "that person does not deserve to be called a theologian [read: a spiritual person] who looks upon the invisible things of God as though they were clearly perceptible in those things that have been made."[37] Where faith is present, God does the seeing. We shut our eyes and are glad to do so, like children praying at bedtime.

This dynamic makes up much of the spiritual content of AA. Perhaps it is for this reason that many AAs report that Step 3 is their "favorite step" and "the most important step." Along these lines, my friend and fellow minister Aaron Zimmerman once told me the following story about himself:

> "I had taken the week off work, and our kids were with their grandparents. My wife and I were really looking forward to our 'staycation': we'd get some good R&R, and also check some things off that long to-do list every homeowner knows all too well.
>
> "Day one was great. Fun, restful, and productive. But that night I found myself filled with anxiety. I couldn't stop thinking about the fact that my vacation would eventually end and I'd have to go back to the office. I love my work, but I was overwhelmed thinking about the sheer amount of *stuff* that loomed in my inbox, the pile of papers on my desk, the events I had to plan…I began to expand my worries beyond my professional life. I began to think about the drama in my extended family. If you have a family, you know what a big mistake *this* was. Eventually, I drifted into shallow sleep, only to wake up with intense pain in my jaw. I had been clenching my teeth all night. The same thing happened the second night. And the third.
>
> Apparently, it takes three days for me to reach desperation. So, finally, I got up, went downstairs, and knelt in my living room. As I prayed, with my eyes

---

[37] Heidelberg Disputation, Thesis 19. Trans. Forde, Gerhard O.

closed, I saw Jesus and me. He was looking at me, and I was looking at him. Or I was trying to. I could barely see over an armload of boulders I was carrying. Each boulder represented a burden in my life, one of my anxieties, stresses or fears. Barely able to hold them, I heard Jesus say, 'Give them to me.'

"I started handing over these enormous stones. As I did, I named each one. Finally, Jesus held them all. I looked at my empty hands. I felt light. I could stand up straight for the first time. I could breathe again.

"When I looked back at Jesus, I noticed that he was beginning to *grow*. And suddenly he was enormous. So enormous, in fact, that these boulders—which had not changed in size *one bit*—were now little pebbles in his hand. He casually put them in his pocket, looked at me, smiled, and walked away. I opened my eyes, went back upstairs, and fell into a sound sleep."

The person who takes Step 3 is like Atlas, finally removing the world from his shoulders, handing it back to the one who holds it upon its axis like a tiny spinning pebble. With this kind of reorientation, the future that once seemed clear now becomes opaque, which is as it should be. What a relief!

"The Actual Taking" of Step 3

"A religious, or spiritual experience, is the act of giving up reliance on one's own omnipotence."
-Dr. Harry Tiebout, psychiatrist and close friend to AA in its early years

It's time for another farm story. This one involves a pig, a chicken, and a cow, who one day decide to show their appreciation to the farmer who takes such exceptional care of them. The pig asks,

"What can we do for the farmer that will convey our gratitude?" After a brief pause, the chicken replies, "I've got it! We'll make him breakfast. I'll provide the eggs. Cow, you can provide the milk. And, Pig, you provide the bacon." The pig immediately responds, "Hold on a second! For you two, giving eggs and milk is not such a big deal, but for me, bacon means putting my whole life on the line." And so it is with the spiritual life in Step 3. There is no room for "a little bit". Either the whole loaf is swallowed, or it is not. As the saying goes, "you cannot be just a little bit pregnant." New life necessarily brings with it the death of the old.

To clarify, the 3rd Step consists of an actual prayer, one in which an individual asks God to take over her life completely from scratch – from top to bottom:

> "God, I offer myself to Thee, to build with me and do with me as Thou wilt. Relieve me of the bondage of self that I may better do Thy will. Take away my difficulties that victory over them may bear witness to those I would help of Thy power, Thy love, and Thy way of life. May I do Thy will always."[38]

Immediately following this famously self-annihilating prayer, the Big Book author writes, "We thought well before taking this step, making sure we were ready; that we could at last abandon ourselves utterly to Him" (63). It's a strange statement, and one wonders if anyone can ever be completely "ready" for anything, let alone the total abandonment of self. But again, the readiness in question actually looks a lot more like exhaustion than preparation. Drowning people grab on to life preservers. The secret to "taking Step 3" lies in the failure of the life that has not taken it. Bill W.

---

[38] Feel free to pray it if you feel so inclined, but read it over first, and consider its implications before you try to put your heart into it.

came to the same insight in Step 3 of *Twelve Steps and Twelve Traditions:*

> "Should his own image in the mirror be too awful to contemplate (and it usually is), he might first take a look at the results normal people are getting from self-sufficiency. Everywhere he sees people filled with anger and fear, society breaking up into warring fragments. Each fragment says to the others, "We are right and you are wrong." Every such pressure group, if it is strong enough, self-righteously imposes its will upon the rest. And everywhere the same thing is being done on an individual basis. The sum of all this mighty effort is less peace and less brotherhood than before. The philosophy of self-sufficiency is not paying off. Plainly enough, it is a bone-crushing juggernaut whose final achievement is ruin." (37)

The Pointer Sisters Know Better

"Son, your life ain't none of your damn business."
-Alabama AA old-timer

As children grow up, their baby teeth fall out. But before they come out, they become loose, which can be irritating for the child. Sometimes parents suggest tying the loose tooth to a door handle using a piece of floss. The parent then tells the child, "Now count to ten. Then I'll slam the door closed and your tooth will be out." The nervous child starts to count (hesitantly) "one…two…three" – when SLAM, Dad pushes the door closed early. The kid screams, "You said you would wait until I counted to 10!" But the parents know that the child never would have gotten there. In a similar way, God often uses Step 3 to curtail the life of self-centeredness that, except in the most severe cases, will work its way out to the very end of someone's life.

The grace of God, in this respect, comes like a thief in the night. It pulls the tablecloth out from under the table settings before much of anything has been put away. God intervenes. *He is not a gentleman; He is a parent.* God is not accepted; he becomes irresistible. Like rowers in a boat filled with holes, the passengers soon find themselves swimming.

Old-timer Chucky T. once said that "people don't change until the pain of staying the same becomes greater than the pain of changing." We recall the pig we read about at the beginning of this section, which depicts people's reluctance to lay their "will and life" on the line. Once this reluctance is overcome, however, a realignment of our perspective occurs. As the Big Book observes, "we become less and less interested in ourselves, our little plans and designs" (63). We are reminded of another great hit from the 80s, this one by the Pointer Sisters: "I'm so excited, I'm so excited! I'm about to lose control and I think I like it."

> *"God, I offer myself to Thee, to build with me and do with me as Thou wilt. Relieve me of the bondage of self that I may better do Thy will. Take away my difficulties that victory over them may bear witness to those I would help of Thy power, Thy love, and Thy way of life. May I do Thy will always."*
> *-Step 3 Prayer*

II: THE HEART OF THE MATTER

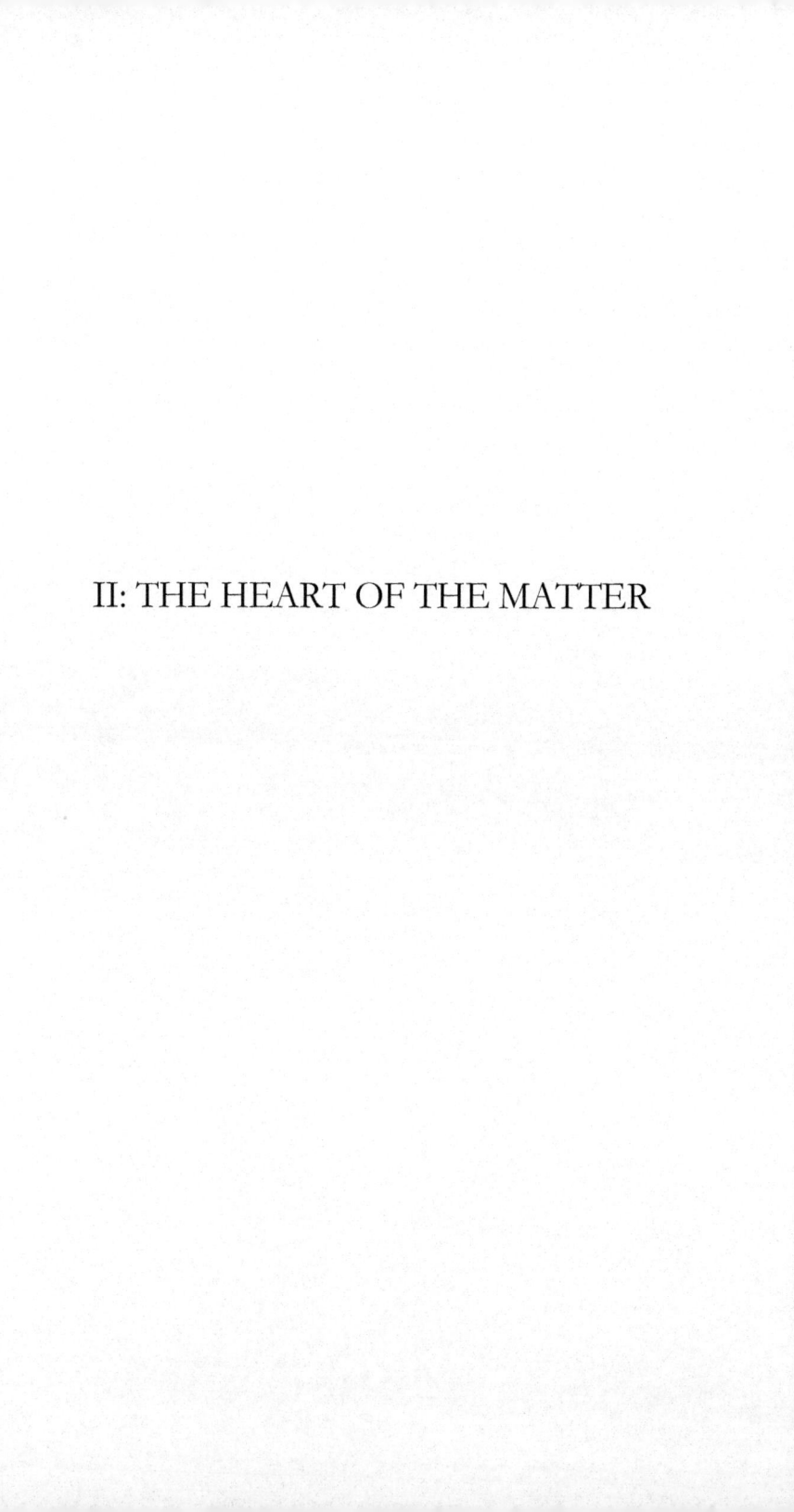

Step 4

"Made a Searching and Fearless Moral Inventory of Ourselves."

"Forgive everyone your sins."
-Jack Kerouac

"Why do you look at the speck of sawdust in your brother's eye and pay no attention to the plank in your own eye?...First take the plank out of your own eye."
-Matthew 7:3-5

Just as the Twelve Steps started with a recognition of our powerlessness over addiction, so too the 4th Step encourages a brutally honest self-examination of our life on a broader scale. The Big Book describes this step as a "personal housecleaning." Imagine a messy room, or worse, a messy house. Picture dirty dishes piled up in the sink, overflowing laundry baskets, piles of old mail, dirty carpet, dust on the ceiling fan blades, burnt out light bulbs in the light fixtures, and cob webs in the corners. Maybe there are socks on the floor, and other items strewn about. Add to this a basement full of abandoned projects, and an attic stuffed to the gills with long-forgotten possessions. And then there are the bathrooms...yuck! This house needs to be cleaned.

AA would suggest that most people's lives require the same sort of upkeep.[39] This is especially true of lives that are in the midst of collapse, as they frequently are when a person arrives at her first AA meeting. Indeed, AA is often the last place people want to end up, or "the last house on the block," as it has been called. Its shabby façade is considerably harder to approach than Mrs. Jones' white picket fence house down the street, which always seems to glisten by comparison.

AA understands that most people's lives are far messier than their houses. Even people with clean homes do not have clean lives, and furthermore, clean houses don't stay clean without continued spit and polish. For this reason, everyone, regardless of their relationship with addiction, can benefit from Step 4, from "taking an inventory of themselves."[40] The knowledge of our own weaknesses and limitations continues to disabuse us of self-reliance, and nowhere is this more apparent than in Step 4.

This step is a writing exercise. It is the step that people in AA rarely complete until they have experienced its alternative – the hollow sobriety that comes from failing to address the inner issues behind alcoholism. That is, the same dynamic applies here that we've discussed already, namely that people don't do Step 4

---

[39] Here we can affirm a famous quote from Socrates: "The unexamined life is not worth living."
[40] The number of clergy, for example, that have never been in any kind of therapy is shocking. They are floating out on their own in many cases, with little to no reflective time in the presence of a wise friend. So many clergy tout "accountability" as being so important, and yet have very little regular practice at it. It is a spiritual axiom/basic premise of this book that: *All people need counsel.*

until they can't keep from doing Step 4 any longer.[41] To quote Robert Capon again: "Of course we must believe; but only because there is nothing left for us to do but believe." People dodge and half-heartedly work Step 4 because it is designed to search out "the flaws in [their] make-up" – not exactly what most of us would consider a good time, but something that becomes necessary. As old-timer Chuck T. once put it, "we are driven to the Twelve Steps…and not in a Cadillac!"

Blockages

"When the spiritual malady is overcome, we straighten out mentally and physically."
-Big Book (64)

Years ago I was part of a swim team. One day, before we jumped in the pool, the coach walked up to me and pushed on a bruise on my arm. He said, "Did that hurt?" It did hurt, but only once he pushed on it. Step 4 works a bit like this, pushing on the bruised places in our lives. It does so in order to heal them. As the Sufi poet Rumi wrote, *"The light can only enter into the wound."* Or, to return to the housekeeping analogy, the cleaning can only be effective if it is applied to a specific mess. So what are the messes that occupy our lives?

---

[41] People do try to skip the less preferable or more demanding steps. Steps 4 & 9 are the ones that are most typically worked only partially or not at all. It is often the case that they are avoided until the gnawing lack of thoroughness and attendant misery of an unfulfilling emotional state in sobriety (called "so-dry-ity", or being "dry") motivates a person to revisit the steps in which he skimped. The Big Book encourages the reader to ask himself, "Have [I] tried to make mortar without sand?" (75).

The Big Book focuses on three universally problematic areas of human weakness: Anger, Fear, and Sex. What a list! Who is exempt from dealing with them?

Bill W. describes their impact: "When harboring such feelings, we shut ourselves off from the sunlight of the spirit" (66). Blockages keep things dark, and they block out the sunlight. They are likened to "spiritual disease" (66). I sometimes like to think of the problems – lingering anger, debilitating fear, and shameful sexual experiences – as being like poison, or like cholesterol in an artery. The 4th Step opens the vein so that the poison can be sucked out… by God. It works like an angioplasty, clearing out the blockages so that the blood can flow to the heart unimpeded.

Each of these blockages describes particular expressions of selfishness, which AA sees as the core problem. Again, as Bill Wilson had it: "selfishness, self-centeredness, that we think is the root of our troubles" (62). Traditional Christian theology uses the word "sin" to describe this condition and, to our way of thinking, the words are almost interchangeable. They describe the angling of the human heart, inclined away from God or, to use famous imagery from St. Augustine, curved in upon its own navel.

To start an inventory, a person can say a little prayer. Many in AA use the following one: "God, help me to be honest. Please show me what it is that you wish for me to see about myself." Others even write the words "God help me to be honest" at the top of every page of their 4th Step. If we adopt the idea that God does the revealing, it makes the whole process flow more smoothly. We take inventory in order to find the things that He would reveal to us. We do not need to muster up a great well of personal insight—we just list what comes to mind.

One side note: the Step 4 inventory is a *written* exercise. For those wanting to do it, just get a legal pad and a pen. There is power in the actual experience of writing the material down on paper with one's own hand, and it is not at all the same thing to try to type an inventory or to do it mentally. This also happens to be the most easily applicable step for non-AA members.

Lingering Anger: You Are Not John McEnroe

Think of a bad mood and the impact it carries. There's an old saying: "The boss yells at the employee, who goes home and fights with his wife. She then scolds her son for not doing his chores, and he runs to his room. On the way up the stairs, he kicks the family dog, who was just lounging on the landing." Anger can have a chain-reaction effect, both within ourselves and in our interactions with other people.

The Step 4 inventory starts by looking at resentment, which the Big Book describes as the "number one offender" when it comes to blockage in recovery (64). Resentment, of course, is any kind of lingering anger – the residue of old hurts, disagreements, and frustrations. Nobody chooses to be angry. We talk about anger being something that "gets the better of us." It is insipid, and it sneaks up on us.

We live in a culture so besieged with anger that it can be very difficult to imagine life without it. And so we try to justify our anger. People talk about things like "healthy anger" and "channeling anger in a productive way." Remember John McEnroe, who was famous for his ability to play better tennis when he was angry? AA whole-heartedly parts ways with this train of thought. In AA there is no such thing as "healthy anger." It is all bad; it is always toxic. In short, you are not John McEnroe.

Step 4 asks us instead to consider whether getting rid of our anger would be more helpful than finding ways to hold on to it. Here in

AA, we find arguably the finest outworking of Jesus' famous teachings in the Sermon on the Mount and elsewhere—admonishments such as the ones to "forgive seventy times seven" and "if a person strikes you on the cheek, turn the other cheek" and "love your enemies."

It makes sense that Step 4's inventory begins with a look at anger and resentment. So how do we find our anger? It's not hard.

Resentments: An Exposé

The Big Book suggests that each individual should begin her 4th Step in the following straightforward manner: "In dealing with resentments, we set them down on paper. We listed people [and] institutions...with whom we were angry" (64). [42] "People" are the individuals toward whom we have lingering anger. We refer to them by name. "Institutions" are groups of people (e.g. professions, corporations, races, or religions).

Whom do you resent? Now we make a list.

We write at the top of the first page of our inventory the word "people" and then underline it. Then, going down the page, we simply list the people we resent: "Martha, Alan, that car salesman, Uncle Jeff, the neighbors…"

A few things need to be said about resentments. First, it's possible to love and resent a person at the same time. A person can both love and resent his child or his spouse, for example. Putting a name on this list does not mean we don't love them, so we try not to let our love for a person hinder our honest

---

[42] Perhaps it goes without saying, but the Twelve Step approach to spirituality implies that such a life is incredibly practical. It involves a direct engagement with life, rather than any kind of transcendence. In AA there is nothing more mystical than love for an enemy or charitable concern for the wellbeing of others.

admission that we resent them too. Along the same lines, we typically resent other people for two types of reasons: either they did something that we resent, or they simply "are" a certain way that we resent. We might resent a co-worker for stealing an account from under our nose, or we might resent him for being loud-mouthed, crass or ugly.

Also, resentment is typically an emotional response to a set of circumstances, not a rational thought. You will commonly "know better" than most of your resentments, especially when they are embarrassing to admit. For example you might have a resentment against "fat people" or "Mexicans" or "people who drive pick-up trucks." But, in spite of the ugliness of the content and your knowing better, those resentments are still inside of you, "renting space in your head" as we say in AA. We write them down anyway. Thoroughness is important. One helpful rule of thumb here is that *the more time you have spent with a person, the greater the chance that you are harboring resentment against them.*

One other common hiccup is the thought, "I don't resent them anymore." Perhaps people get over some of their past anger, but usually such statements reflect wishful thinking. Anger lingers – that's the problem. It doesn't tend to go away until a therapeutic process like Step 4 has been undertaken. Common wisdom has it that "time heals all wounds," but AA does not agree. God heals wounds by enabling people to forgive their offenders; otherwise, wounds stay put. Anger typically festers and infects, and not the other way around. This is why resentment is the "number one offender."

There are usually between 5 and 20 key players at any one time in a person's resentful state of mind. For the alcoholic, that number tends to be greater. But it's fair to say that the bulk of one's resentment is focused on just a handful of situations, and the names of between 5 and 10 individuals will comprise most of someone's anger. Every honest list includes at least one or two family members or loved ones. My sponsor once asked me, "John, am I on your list?" I answered, "No", to which he replied, "When are you going to start getting honest?"

In terms of order, we generally find it helpful to start with the present and slowly work our way back through our lives. Those who want to try Step 4 on for size can use the following guidelines; others will simply find them informative. Ask yourself who or what circumstances have caused you anxiety. Whom do you have a problem with? Whom do you not like? Have there been any fights? Write those people down. Start by thinking about your family and your living situation. Think about your job. Bosses and coworkers often find a place on this list. So do neighbors. Then think about your extended family, friends, spouses of friends, and former friends. Remind yourself about the places you've lived and the places you've worked. Are there any other key events from the past that have proved decisive for you in some negative way? Who was involved? Try to reflect in a somewhat objective fashion.

Aim for coming up with between ten and twenty names. It shouldn't take more than fifteen minutes, and the bulk of the names will make your list in a much shorter time than that.

In order to be thorough, also make a list of "institutions" on the same page if there's still room on the right-hand side, or on another page if not. What groups of people do you resent? Do you have any strong political or religious beliefs? They tend to offer plenty of fresh names. And how do you feel about the IRS, cops, different races, rich people, poor people, cat owners, different colleges, certain neighborhoods, or sports teams? Who has wronged you, let you down, or frustrated your goals? Where do you see injustice that affects you on a personal level? Whom do you not want to be associated with? Add them to your list under the "institutions" heading.

STEP 4

It's not hard to find resentments when you start to look for them. It might even seem like you are opening Pandora's Box. The good thing about an inventory is that you can do it at any time; names can always be added. It's important not to get too bogged down trying to make the list "completely complete." That would be impossible.[43]

I remember one individual in AA who showed me a list with over 900 names on it. It was pages and pages of names, the kind of extreme behavior that alcoholics are known for. I wondered if he would ever be able to finish his inventory. We started to look through it together, and I immediately noticed multiple repeats. He had his mom on there about twelve times, and many other individuals were listed multiple times. I remember asking him, "How many Dianes do you know?" Together, we were able to boil his list down to a much more manageable – though still somewhat unwieldy – two hundred and fifty resentments.

At one point, while looking at his section on institutions, I asked him, "It says here that you resent 'communism.' Is that true? Do you really have a resentment toward communism?" He replied, "I guess not." And so we crossed it off the list. I then asked him, "What about 'capitalism?' Is that a big red-button topic for you?" He again said no and we crossed it off the list too. Finally, I perplexedly asked, "What about 'Subaru?' It says here that you resent 'Subaru.' Do you really resent 'Subaru?'" He looked at me with fire in his eyes and responded, "Big time!" Subaru stayed on the list, and we went from there. He was very diligent, and soon we were on to his 5th Step

---

[43] As a young monk Martin Luther almost drove himself insane worrying about the sins he had committed that he couldn't remember. At the time, he believed that he had to confess them in order to receive forgiveness for them. He knew himself well enough to know that he could never finish the job satisfactorily. You can probably imagine how happy he was to discover that God is in the business of picking up this kind of slack.

Most non-alcoholics don't err in his direction though. They tend to put too few names on their list, barely scratching the surface. They are reluctant to acknowledge their resentments because it makes them uncomfortable. To be clear, a cursory attempt at inventory won't do anyone much good. More is better than less. But even fifteen names will get at the material that most needs to be addressed.

The Big Book points out that "staying sore" was "as far as most of us ever got" (66). Just making a list does little for one's mental and spiritual health. If anything, it disturbs it, stirring up the silt at the bottom of the stream and making things murky. For this reason, people sometimes (read: often) find that, when working on their 4th Step, they become irritable in a way that is somewhat uncharacteristic. One friend even spoke of a string of nightmares that plagued him until he had finished his 5th Step. While we neither worry about the agitation nor tell newcomers to expect it, some disturbance during the 4th Step is natural. The most important thing is to finish the inventory,[44] because the peace that lies on the other side of the 4th and 5th Steps is the sort that people would do well not to miss.

If Someone Steps on Your Toe, Say 'Excuse Me'

A wise sponsor once offered his new sponsee the above heading to think about. At first, this statement confused the new AA. What on earth did it mean? He mulled it over. The more he reflected upon it, the more it began to make sense. In order to see himself from a spiritual angle, he needed to see the part he played in causing offense. He wasn't as much of a target in other people's minds as he thought. Instead, he was simply oblivious of how his

---

[44] Alcoholics who start the 4th Step but don't finish it commonly relapse.

behavior in the world was impacting the lives of others, forcing them into uncomfortable situations where they were forced to react suddenly or harshly to him, thereby stepping on his proverbial toe. He was offended, therefore, for many things he had brought upon himself. Once he began to consider this, he began to get a better grasp of how his selfishness had manifested itself in his life. The final portion of inventorying resentment follows this introspective trajectory.

Bill W. writes, "We turned back to the list, for it held the key to the future. We were prepared to look at it from an entirely different angle" (66). The different angle involves finally looking at yourself, rather than continuing to fixate upon the people on your list. It is at this moment, with the list in hand, that one does well to remember Jesus' words: "Why do you look at the speck in your brother's eye and disregard the plank in your own eye?" We now try to look into our own eyes, to see our part. Here is how the Big Book introduces its version of this radical idea:

> "Referring to our list again. Putting out of our minds the wrongs others had done, we resolutely looked for our own mistakes. Where had we been selfish, dishonest, self-seeking and frightened? Though a situation had not been entirely our fault, we tried to disregard the other person involved entirely. Where were we to blame? The inventory was ours, not the other man's. When we saw our faults we listed them. We placed them before us in black and white. We admitted our wrongs honestly..." (67)

"Where were *we* to blame?" The goal now is to identify the part we have played in the resentment. Here we give each name on our list its own page.

We write the name of the person or institution at the top of the page, with "My part?" below it. Then we answer the question, asking ourselves things like, "In what ways have I been contributing to the battle with the person on my list? Did I break his arm? Have I screamed back when she accosted me? Or have I gossiped about him in an attempt to get others on my side? Have I tried in some way to make that person's life more difficult? Have I seen to it that she got fired? If nothing else, *have I been actively averse to the idea of forgiving the person for their wrongdoing?*[45] Have I hypocritically done the same things to others that the person on my list has done to me?" This focus on our part is the side of the resentment that deserves attention. It has most likely been neglected.

The following example should help to illustrate how this works. Imagine a guy named Gary and another guy named Levar. Gary and Levar are not great friends, but they are – or rather used to be – acquaintances. Now they hate each other.

Here's what happened. Both Gary and Levar are smokers. One day Gary found himself sitting next to Levar in the library at their college. Gary noticed that Levar had a fresh pack of cigarettes sticking out of an open zipper pocket in his backpack, and since Gary was fresh out of smokes, he asked Levar if he could bum a cigarette. Somewhat surprisingly, Levar said no, mentioning something about how the price of cigarettes had gotten astronomical and he couldn't afford to spare any. Gary thought this response was ridiculous and stingy. And he didn't expect it.[46]

After mulling it over for a few minutes, Gary decided that Levar's answer was so inappropriate that he would not accept it. He decided it would actually be helpful to Levar to experience one

---

[45] This one question is crucial in instances where the inventory writer has been the victim of some form of abuse (e.g., sexual) that has left behind the residue of deep hurt.

[46] Another great AA slogan: "An expectation is a pre-meditated resentment."

slight punitive consequence for his miserliness, even if only the cosmos noticed. While Levar's back was turned, Gary snuck up behind his chair and slowly reached into Levar's open backpack, pulling the exposed pack out of the open pocket. At the moment he was removing a single cigarette, Levar sensed something going on just behind him. Levar turned around suddenly, catching Gary in the act of stealing the cigarette, the pack still in his hand.

To the surprise of everyone, Levar screamed out an expletive and pulled out a meat cleaver from the inside of his blazer. In a single swooping motion, the cleaver sliced through Gary's forearm. Gary's severed hand fell to the ground, still clutching the pack. Levar had cut off Gary's hand.

That was five years ago, but understandably, the resentment against Levar was still alive in Gary's mind. Hatred for Levar seethed in him whenever he looked at the stump that used to be his hand.

Let's look at Gary's inventory. When asked about his resentment toward Levar, Gary easily rattles off a list of reasons that justify his hatred. Due to Levar's disproportionate response to the situation, Gary has felt for years that his anger was well-founded. Nonetheless, that anger was robbing him of peace, and as far as AA was concerned, it was blocking out "the sunlight of the spirit". To quote an old Taoist sage, Gary's resentment "is a rock in his stream of consciousness." Step 4 is designed to help Gary get past his resentment at Levar.

This is what Gary's inventory looks like:

I'm resentful at: LEVAR

My part?

-I didn't respect his "No" to my request.
-I tried to steal his cigarettes.

-I have been trying to make other people hate Levar, too, by getting them to take my side and by gossiping about him.
-I have not wanted to forgive him.
-Sometimes I don't like to share either.
-I would be angry too if someone tried to steal from me.
-Smoking is unhealthy and not getting to smoke is not really a bad thing.

With the help of the inventory, Gary finally glimpsed his part in the resentment. Had he not tried to steal a cigarette after he was told he could not have one, he would still have an arm today. Although he found Levar's stinginess outrageous, he had to admit that he sometimes refuses simple requests himself. With these important insights, Gary learned that he too was to blame for what happened. The long-standing resentment began to lose a little of its steam.

A few more quick tips for the would-be inventory taker: First, it is easy to start with the situations or people where your part is most glaring, and then work on the ones where you feel stuck. If need be, a sponsor or mentor can help you see your part. If you knock out five each night, it should be easy to finish this part of an inventory by the end of a single week.[47]

---

[47] Like exercise, this kind of work rarely happens if you don't schedule the time to do it. Try to keep the ball rolling by doing a minimum of two names or institutions each day. If it's not coming easily and you have a long list, schedule a time where you can spend a few hours uninterruptedly knocking out the entire inventory. Only very seldom will the actual writing require more than a few hours. Set a deadline for your 5th Step, where you will meet with another person to discuss what you've written down. Then, if need be, binge away the night before, coffee in hand. I wrote most of my first inventory in an airport on the way home to meet my sponsor, the night before our scheduled 5th Step. I had put it off for too long.

While each case is, to some extent, different from the next, there are few (if any) resentments that will not reveal some element of your own culpability. Seeing anger from this angle almost never happens naturally, and it will often be hard for us to find "our part" when we first start writing. Learning to write inventory is a bit like learning to ride a bike.

One other side note: In an inventory, we often find that what we write down about "our part" is repetitive. And it should be. Our less admirable qualities tend to manifest themselves in a pattern. Sponsors commonly urge inventory takers not to worry about the repetition, but simply to write it down again. No new insights are required for each name on the list. In fact, it is worth hitting ourselves in the head with the same hammer multiple times. Maybe it will jog some of the self-centeredness loose.

"Pray for the S.O.B." (Classic AA Saying)

"This is a sick man. How can I be helpful to him? God save me from being angry. Thy will be done."
-Big Book (67)

The foreign nature of the moral inventory points to its divine origin. Forgiveness comes from God, and it tends to be most rare in the situations where it is most needed.

For this reason, the Big Book encourages us to pray the following prayer — not only when we are taking written inventory, but also in all other times when anger rises to the surface of our thoughts and feelings: *"This is a sick person. How can I be helpful to him or her? God save me from being angry. Thy will be done."* The prayer is powerful for at least three reasons.

First, in acknowledging the "sick"-ness of the person toward whom our anger is directed, we are encouraged to have a bit of understanding. Our goal, as the author reminds us, is to show our enemy "the same tolerance, pity, and patience that we would cheerfully grant a sick friend" (67). Understanding and compassion go hand in hand, after all; you can't have one without the other. This is why the best mental illness counselors are often those who have struggled themselves. To the extent that we are aware our own limitations, we tend to find that we have compassion for others in those exact areas. Associating a person's misdeeds with the symptoms of illness, rather than with willful wrongdoing, is a healthy mental leap. Jesus led the charge for this move with his famous refrain: "It is not the healthy who need a doctor, but the sick. I did not come for the righteous, but for sinners" (Mk 2:17, cf. Mt 9:12-13).

Second, the prayer suggests that we focus our attention on how we can be helpful to the person whom we resent. What could be further from our minds when it comes to someone we hate? In this way, the prayer forms a point of contact with Jesus' exhortation to "Love your enemies" (Mt 5:44). By considering how we might be helpful, the abstract becomes concrete, and we are given a useful direction in which we can head. We focus on the ways we can serve.

Sometimes a philosophical framework can help us figure out the way in which we should act. If we have a goal in mind, we can determine a course of action in light of that overarching theme. So it is with anger; we seek to be helpful in the moment when we are feeling angry. This opens us up to God's inspiration while simultaneously closing our eyes to the frustrated, less-than-productive elements of our own thinking. In so doing, it breaks the normal monologue of criticism which goes through our minds whenever we're around the person we resent. We don't have to know specifically what to say or what we want to do when we're around that person. Instead, we simply pray that God will show us how we can be helpful. Then we keep our eyes open. This approach can usually get us through an unexpected situation with a difficult person. As the Big Book affirms, "It works – it really does" (88).

Finally, the prayer seeks God's help with anger. In an instant, it enables us to accept our own inability to rid ourselves of anger, and it seeks the one who can. The prayer puts the onus on God, which is the great secret to the spiritual life. It takes the weight off of our shoulders. We are reminded that we are powerless over our anger, and that we need help to be rid of it. In Christian terms, it is a prayer of repentance, and one which therefore opens us to God's volition. Praying for God to save us from our anger and to show us how we can serve the people we resent soon becomes a regular part of our thought-life – if, that is, we have become honestly convinced of resentment's futility. No anger is good anger.

Fear

"I'm your boogie man"
-KC and the Sunshine Band

When my wife and I first moved to Charleston we befriended a newly married, very sweet couple who lived nearby. But this couple was also extremely timid, as shy as any two people we had ever met before. It occurred to us that they were a perfect match for each other. On a related note, my wife and I like to throw an annual Easter brunch blow-out. We invite our friends together to share in the joys of that momentous holiday. So when it came time to send out invites, our timid neighbors were included on the list. Rather than mailing the letter, my wife asked me to deliver the invitation by hand.

So I headed down the street one evening to hand off the invitation and say hello. I climbed their steps and rang the doorbell. Just behind the door I could hear the sound of their television. In response to the bell, their dogs began barking and gathered in the foyer. But nobody came to the door. I rang the bell again, and shouted: "Hey y'all, it's your neighbor, John. Just wanted to drop off an invitation." Still no answer. But I could see the couple's shoes huddled together on the living room coffee table, frozen through the blinds. I tried the bell again with no luck and eventually left the invitation in the mailbox.

It occurred to me as I walked home that they had once mentioned that a neighborhood fellow had knocked on their door, entreating them to give him some money. They had mentioned that in response, they no longer opened their door to unexpected strangers. While I in no way fit into that category, their fears had categorized me as a threat. I had come bearing good news, warmth, and an invitation to a party. But they could not receive my call.

The story illustrates the impact that fear has upon life. It blocks out possibility. It stifles the unanticipated, even in the case of the good. It ascribes a negative value to unknowns – which are as much a fact of life, if not more so, than the things of which we are certain.

While resentment may be the "number one offender" when it comes to spiritual blockage, fear is not far behind. The text points out that "this short word touches about every aspect of our lives…the fabric of our existence was shot through with it" (67-68). It's an unfortunate fact. In the same way that we do not wish to defend "healthy anger", we also do not wish to defend fear, though its necessity cannot altogether be denied. We think that less fear, or at least less anxiety and worry, is almost always a good thing.

As with anger, the Big Book suggests that we need God to remove our fears, that we cannot rid ourselves of them. It is no wonder that Jesus spent a substantial portion of the Sermon on the Mount addressing this one issue. He too saw fear getting in the way of a person's trust in God.[48]

The Big Book suggests that we first "review our fears thoroughly. We put them on paper" (64). At the top of a new page, then, we write, "Fears" and underline it. Next, under the heading, we simply list our fears, even the ones we know are irrational. Are we afraid of spiders, of walking down the stairs in the dark or of needles or giving blood? Fears often concern the future, because that's where they live. Perhaps we're convinced that we might suddenly lose our job or that something terrible will happen to one of our children. Are we afraid of having an online presence or of identity theft? In truth, it is possible to be afraid of anything. We briefly list each fear that comes to mind

Where fear exists, usually a harmful attempt to master that fear – via control – is also found. For example, people who are

---

[48] Jesus' famous passage about fear, taken from the sixth chapter of Matthew's Gospel:

"Therefore I tell you, do not worry about your life, what you will eat or drink; or about your body, what you will wear. Is not life more than food, and the body more than clothes? Look at the birds of the air; they do not sow or reap or store away in barns, and yet your heavenly Father feeds them. Are you not much more valuable than they? Can any one of you by worrying add a single hour to your life?

"And why do you worry about clothes? See how the flowers of the field grow. They do not labor or spin. Yet I tell you that not even Solomon in all his splendor was dressed like one of these. If that is how God clothes the grass of the field, which is here today and tomorrow is thrown into the fire, will he not much more clothe you—you of little faith? So do not worry, saying, 'What shall we eat?' or 'What shall we drink?' or 'What shall we wear?' For the pagans run after all these things, and your heavenly Father knows that you need them. But seek first his kingdom and his righteousness, and all these things will be given to you as well. Therefore do not worry about tomorrow, for tomorrow will worry about itself. Each day has enough trouble of its own (vv. 25-34).

afraid of the dark won't go to sleep unless the light is left on in their rooms. And people who fear social situations or potentially awkward conversations will typically make silly excuses about why they cannot attend various social events. Similarly, the ability to consider any kind of a move (be it professional, locale-related, or even just down the street) is usually infested by the baleful impact of corrosive fears. They hinder our ability to engage with the possibility that God is driving our lives.

We find ourselves wanting to seek a new, spiritual approach to dealing with fear only after the failure of our own futile concoctions and tired methods becomes apparent to us. How well are your methods for dealing with fear working for you? Have your attempts to grapple with fear cut you off from the world at large? With regard to fear the Big Book asks one key question: "We asked ourselves why we had [these fears]. *Wasn't it because self-reliance had failed us?*" (68)

Until we see how this question relates to our fears, we will miss the thrust of Step 4's insight. The author is pointing out that we have fears to the exact extent that our attempts to control the undesirable aspects of life have "failed us." *To the extent that we can't control something that we don't like, we fear it.*

In taking an inventory of our fears, it is worth noting the ways in which they have been controlling our behavior in affected areas. We reflect upon the impact of each fear upon our lives. Do any patterns of avoidance reveal themselves? In what ways do we compensate for our fears? We write these consequences down in parentheses after the related fear has been listed. If we need more room, we give each fear on the list its own page. Some discover that fear has been hindering many areas of their lives, much in the same way that resentment does. Unchecked fear can cause a person to walk through life with the spiritual equivalent of a devastating limp. It prevents, blocks, and binds us. Yet there is "a better way" (68).

Fear's Antidote: "Better Men Than We Are Using It Constantly" (85)

A very cool little horror movie called *Don't Be Afraid of the Dark* came out in 2011. It tells the story of a little girl whose family moves into an old house. She hears voices at night, calling to her and luring her down to the basement. Soon it becomes apparent that something ancient and supernatural is living in the house, and more importantly, that "it" is after this little girl. As the movie unfolds, we finally see the adversary: a bunch of tiny little creatures that feed on the teeth of children. In one scene the poor girl is attacked by a team of them while she is taking a bath in a claw foot tub. They climb up through the old house's air ducts, shut off the lights, and then swarm the tub. The movie was criticized by many reviewers for one main reason; it's a horror movie in which the horror turns out to be something that is not very scary when it is brought into the light. Little creatures just don't incite doom. In fact, they're almost cute.

In a related and rather well-known passage from the *12 & 12*, Bill W. describes how fears "turn out to be bogeymen" (49). He suggests that most fears, when actually confronted, turn out to be illusory. It's more than what happens with the not-so-scary-after-all "faerie-folk" in *Don't Be Afraid of the Dark*; it's that they turn out to be imaginary, possessing no actual content. Like bogeymen under the bed, we find that – in truth – there is nothing there at all.

Moreover, our problem is less *that* we fear and more that we don't seem to fear the *right* things at the right times. We miscalculate, and consequently we punish ourselves with the exact measures we think will protect us. As Christie Barnes, author of *The Paranoid Parents Guide* (and mother of four), points out: "We are constantly overestimating rare dangers while underestimating common ones."[49] Such is the nature of self-reliance, especially when it is applied to the arena of fear.

The Big Book approach to dealing with fear suggests, as it always does, that we seek God's aid. Fear is just like any other issue – something characterized by the need for God's intervention. To the extent that fear gets in the way of the living of our life, we are encouraged to pray that God will remove it. We'll explore this dynamic in much greater detail in Steps 6 and 7, but the Big Book explicitly introduces this theme into the material in Step 4. With regard to fear, the text tells us:

> "We are now on a different basis [i.e., in wake of Step 3)]; the basis of trusting and relying upon God. We trust infinite God rather than our finite selves. We are in the world to play the role He assigns. Just to the extent that we do as we think He would have us, and humbly rely on Him, does He enable us to match calamity with serenity… We can laugh at those who think spirituality the way of weakness. Paradoxically, it is the way of strength. The verdict of the ages is that faith means courage. All men of faith have courage. They trust their God…we let Him demonstrate, through us, what He can do. *We ask Him to remove our fear and direct our attention to what He would have us be.* At once, we commence to outgrow fear." (68)

Did you spot the prayer? "We ask Him to remove our fear and direct our attention to what He would have us be."

To reiterate, a spiritual awakening enables a person to face fear – not avoid it. I recently had the privilege of taking a man who worked for a pest control company through the Twelve Steps. At

---

[49] Lisa Belkin, "Keeping Kids Safe from the Wrong Dangers", *The New York Times*, September 18, 2010, http://www.nytimes.com/.

one point, as we discussed fears, it became apparent that his job had required him to face many of the things in life that most people dodge at all costs: rats, cellars, dank and dark crawlspaces, spiders, bats, cockroaches, and other common phobias. Not surprisingly, he had a smaller list of fears on his inventory than most people do. At one point, after I had tried to help him discover one or two common areas of fear to no avail, he said, "I think I've got one: I'm afraid to buy a motorcycle. If I got one, I think I would get hooked on speeding!" What else could I say but, "That's a good one. Put it down on the list as your third fear." Then I told him to spend a week seeing if God brought anything else to mind. A few more were added, but not many.

Of course, in comparison with most others, his resentments were off the charts! But in the arena of fear he was already a great portrait of spirituality. He told me about the time early in his career when, after learning what was involved in ridding a house of termites, he refused to go under a house. He soon realized that he either had to get over that fear or pursue a new line of work. Grow or go, right? The results were self-evident, for he had much to teach me. Today he collects poisonous spiders for fun.

Most people, when they're finally given the ability to face the crippling nature of their fears, find that praying for God to remove them comes quite naturally.[50] Unlike my friend in pest control, most people are unable to teach themselves to face their fears without using a prayerful approach. While he had been able to confront his fears on his own (in a most uncharacteristic fashion), he was in desperate need of God's help with his temper. Our point is that, where character is concerned, no one is exempt from the need for spiritual help, although the symptoms may vary a bit from one person to the next.

---

[50] The 6th Step describes this state of mind as being "entirely ready to have God remove" our fear.

"Let's Talk About Sex" (George Michael)

"Now about sex. Many of us needed an overhauling there."
-Big Book (68)

Sex is the great taboo. It makes people bristle. Talk of sex and the feelings of anger and guilt that frequently accompany it keep more people away from church than any other single issue. In social situations, the topic of sex tends to polarize more quickly than almost any other, perhaps beating out both religion and politics. What is AA's stance on sexual disputes? "We want to stay out of this controversy" (69).

While many of us are quick to take positions on matters related to sex in general, very few people are willing to talk about their personal sex lives openly. This is understandable given the broad spectrum of strongly-held opinions concerning sexual ethics. Everyone holds to some personal standard of sexual conduct; we punish others to the extent that their behavior deviates from our personally held ideal. It should come as no surprise that sexual baggage makes up a huge percentage of the material that lurks in the closets, basements, and attics of the human psyche. While "sex problems" seems ambiguous, we like it that way: in our definition, anything producing shame or emotional dissonance in one's sexual history is a concern that should be aired and addressed.

A housecleaning on this front is almost always crucial. The 4th Step is in no way caught off guard by our checkered sexual histories. In fact, it expects them: "We all have sex problems. We'd hardly be human if we didn't" (69).

It is remarkable that the hysteria that surrounds the subject of sex in our culture is almost entirely absent in the world of AA. There are two reasons for this. First, AA seeks to provide alcoholics with a non-judgmental environment. The attractiveness of an AA group, especially for a newcomer, largely depends upon this one virtue. Where sex is concerned, this is particularly true. The Big Book is both aware of the extreme opinions that punctuate all conversations related to sex, and it is quick to state: "We do not wish to be the arbiters of anyone's sex conduct" (69).

The second reason for AA's relatively calm sexual conversation is its view that sex is just like any other problem. In AA, all sin carries the same rank: it's all rooted in the same deviation from loving God to loving the self. The moment people begin to draw lines of deviation between one sin and another, either by ranking them in terms of severity or by attempting to draw a distinction between motive and behavior, they get into impossibly complex theological material. AA's approach lines up nicely with Paul's sentiment in Romans 3:23: "all have sinned and fallen short of the glory of God." And AA firmly believes that all problems straighten out when cast under God's dominion. Matters of sex, just like anything else, fall under the scrutiny of God; they do not have to fall under the scrutiny of the group. In other words, nagging is not required for change to occur. You might say that sex, and all other moral matters, are viewed as "secondary" issues in AA. In this context, conventional morality pales by comparison to the life-or-death issues of drinking and the working of the Twelve Steps.

Again, in AA there is really only one thing that takes on a moral dimension: the working or not working of the Twelve Steps. If you are sober and not working the Twelve Steps, then you are doing something wrong. If you are working the Twelve Steps, then all the other issues will fall into place in God's time. Again we quote the Big Book: "When the spiritual malady is overcome, we straighten out mentally and physically." And sexually, for that matter (64).

While outsiders may have a problem with this approach, they cannot argue with the empirical evidence, which is that it works – and that it works better than what one finds in most churches. In AA we find a group of people who are perhaps more honest, as a group, about matters of sex than any other. The people of AA talk about sex problems without excuse, and they deal with their sex problems accordingly. This approach works so well because AA understands that sex problems do not simply bow down to right judgment, willpower, or conventional knowing-better. God's help is the only factor that can turn the tide of self-interest and compulsion.

The result is that, in fact, the sober individuals of AA have more transparency, less shame and secrecy, and more stories of growth and healing when it comes to their sex lives than most Christian believers. Far too many churches have become places where people go to hide from the reality of their own sexual shame, where any kind of honesty about one's sexual past is discouraged by fear of judgment. AA's lack of condemnation, on the other hand, produces a lack of sublimation, which in turn leads to healthier and more spiritual sex lives.

How to Take Inventory of One's Sex Life

Obviously any inventory of one's sex life involves making "a review of our own [sex] conduct over the years past" (69). Most of us simply need to record a list of names, just as with resentments and fears. If the name is not remembered but the circumstances are, a dummy-name that jogs the memory will do fine (e.g., "girl in Athens" or, "one-night-stand"). If there are any especially embarrassing or painful incidences (e.g. molestation or abuse), we include them too. We start with the present and move backwards, including ourselves on the list last.

After the list has been made, each name is then given its own section to be prayerfully analyzed with the help of the following questions: *"Where had we been selfish, dishonest, or inconsiderate? Whom had we hurt? Did we unjustifiably arouse jealousy, suspicion or bitterness? Where were we at fault, what should we have done instead?"* (69).

It is important to note if any patterns emerge. Odds are that we have repeatedly acted in selfish ways where sex is concerned. What are they? How have we caused harm? Have we led people on or sent mixed messages? If it would be awkward to suddenly bump into one of the people on our list, why is this the case? What did we do that created the awkwardness? What was our part? Maybe we said we would call and then didn't?

We put these answers down on paper in order to shape "our future sex ideal." What goals for the future arise from these considerations? The book encourages us to "shape a sane and sound ideal for our future sex life" and then to pray that God will help us to live up to it as we move into the future (69). For many Christians, abstinence outside of marriage will be the goal.

We commonly find that where honesty, compassion, and thoughtfulness have been present, harm will not have been done. The 4th Step is where we look for the absence of these attributes and how our selfishness has robbed us of our usefulness to our fellow human beings. By pinpointing our destructive patterns and the misery they have caused, we may find that God begins to shape us in ways that do not arouse shame, guilt, and the feeling of being blocked off from Him.

Finally

"Can you see that this death of self is not, in the final analysis, something you can do?"
-G. Forde, *"Sermon on the Death of Self"*

At this point, we should have a little journal or notepad with a fair amount of writing in it. Resentments, fears, and sexual issues have been listed and analyzed. We are now ready for Step 5.[51]

There may be places where we feel that we have been "stuck" in our reflections. But we need not worry about this if we've made an honest attempt and tried to work through the material in the way that has been laid out above. To the extent that something important is missing, the person to whom we divulge this material in the 5th Step will likely be able to help us connect the dots.

Sometimes in AA, the writing of a perfect "by the book, 4-column inventory" is overly emphasized. There is no such thing as a perfect 4th Step inventory. The Big Book offers great insight and guidance, but it makes room for error in its execution. In the same way that the exact wording of the 3rd Step prayer is inconsequential so long as the correct sentiment is expressed (63), we know that it is not perfect adherence to directions that brings sobriety and sanity, but God's grace.[52]

---

[51] The *12 & 12* adds matters of family and money to the list of things that should be looked at in the 4th Step. If you have particular discomfort in one of those two areas, you might also do a similar review of your situation in that respect. As always, the important thing is to list honestly the problematic areas and the faulty ways in which we have added to these difficulties.

[52] This is a point that is often missed by the zealous newcomer who has found freedom and release from sin through the Twelve Steps. The Steps point to God, but they are not synonymous with Him. We do well to remember Jesus' relevant (and mind-blowingly insightful) words: "The Sabbath [Twelve Steps] was made for man, not man for the Sabbath [Twelve Steps]" (Mk 2:27).

The purpose of the 4th Step inventory is to confront our shortcomings as God reveals them to us. When that has happened, we are prepared for the next three steps.

But before we move on, we might ask what exactly our role in writing the inventory has been. Take the example of a new AA or, better yet, someone outside the world of addiction who has just finished an inventory along the lines of Step 4. She's substantially overhauled her perspective, possibly for the first time in her life. Hopefully she has looked at all kinds of primary situations in her life from new angles. Honesty has been paramount, and many lurking suspicions, formerly denied, have probably become evident. To quote the Big Book, she has "swallowed and digested some big chunks of truth about [herself]" (71). How has our 4th Step practitioner suddenly been able to see things about herself that she's never been able to see before? In my own case, looking back, it seemed much more like God had helped me do this 4th Step work, and that, apart from His help, it would never have been done. Sometimes in AA, people say things like, "you put the pen to the paper, and then God does the writing." I wholly sympathize with that interpretation of the inventory process.

Consider the following story: Years ago, in a particularly stuck period of my sobriety, I sought the help of a therapist. Picture the quintessential wise, New York City Jewish therapist. This man had a renowned reputation for helping Christian ministers, and I was very eager to receive his help in dealing with my life as it then stood.

In our first session, on a Monday morning, I told him about myself: my confusion about the future (especially vis-à-vis career), frustrations in my romantic life, and my voracious appetite for clothes and shopping. I voiced too the difficulties I was having with basic aspects of adult responsibility. At one point, I think I told him that I hated "the post office." At the end of our time, I asked him if there was anything I could do in the next week to make the most of the therapy.

He said, "Before you come back next week, I want you to buy a stamp."

The following Monday morning I returned to his office, stamp in hand. I walked into the office practically waving it in front of his face, but he didn't seem eager to give it much attention.

At the end of that second session, I again asked the same thing:

"What do you want me to do this week?"

He replied, "This week, I want you to buy a post card."

The next week I came in with a "Greetings from Chinatown" postcard I had picked up on the street near my apartment.

He responded, "Good. Next week I want you to put the stamp on the post card."

I returned the following week to show him my postcard, now with the stamp affixed in the upper right-hand corner. At the end of our session, I asked again,

"What do you want me to do?"

"Write something on the post card," he told me.

A week later I walked in, feeling a bit blue. I told him forthrightly that I had not written anything on the postcard and showed him the blank front. He responded in a way that surprised me.

Dryly, and with a slight smile, he replied, "That's okay; all I ever wanted you to do was buy a stamp."

I had assumed that I had ceased to make any progress because I had stopped doing the things he wanted me to do. To the contrary, he was suggesting that the therapeutic work that had begun with our meetings was far bigger than my ability to stop it.

Once I had purchased a stamp, I was "dead in the water" of forward progress.

I never asked him for an assignment again. By the time I finished meeting with him a few months later, I had decided to enter the ordained ministry, enrolled in a seminary in England, and – most importantly – met and started dating the woman who would become my wife. Something had indeed begun to move in my life, and the fruits were undeniable.

And so it is with the 4th Step inventory. Once a newcomer has made her resentment list, I now smile to myself because I know that the proverbial "stamp" has already been purchased. The inventory process usually bumps into hurdles at some point, but they are easily overcome with the help of an unflappable sponsor. If the subject is given space, the potent cocktail of personal discomfort and God's grace typically works wonders in motivating a return to the work.[53]

---

[53] As previously mentioned, people often balk on the 4th Step. The inventory experience is *that* unpleasant. The goal of the sponsor here is to help make the experience as easy as possible for the inventory taker. For sponsors, it may be helpful to schedule a time for the subject to meet with you, where he can quietly do the writing in your presence, like a kind of 4th Step "study hall." Usually people don't do this work until they become convinced that they cannot find peace until they do it. This means that discomfort plays a crucial role. The sponsor does not need to increase the subject's feelings of discomfort, except for gently asking, "How is the inventory coming along?" You might relay your own experience of procrastination with the work. It will be written when the time is right and the pain of not writing it surpasses the pain of doing it.

Step 5

"We Admitted to God, to Ourselves, and to Another Human Being the Exact Nature of Our Wrongs"

"You're only as sick as your secrets."
-Unknown

"We pocket our pride and go to it, illuminating every twist of character, every dark cranny of the past."
-Big Book (75)

The Twelve Steps are "ego-deflators." They typically direct us in the opposite direction of our instincts.[54] In no case is this more evident than with Step 5, which involves bringing another person

---

[54] In that sense, we do well to acknowledge that the spiritual impulse is not a self-generated phenomenon. Perhaps it is even divinely inspired (i.e., to the exact extent that it is counter-intuitive). We'll discuss this more in Steps 6 & 7.

in on the nasty truth about ourselves that has surfaced in the 4th Step inventory. As long as someone refuses to share his Step 4 inventory, to an extent, he is trying to hang onto his past and deal with it independently. By sharing our histories, however, it's like we take a poison within ourselves and distribute it over a much larger body. Step 5 reduces the damaging impact of our past by sharing it with a sponsor. This is where the skeletons come out of the closet so that they can receive a proper burial.

The Big Book is quick to point out that the 4th Step is not a cure in and of itself: "in actual practice many of us found that a solitary self-appraisal is insufficient" (72). In other words, the 4th Step is simply a diagnosis. Like all humbling self-knowledge, it provides no ameliorating salve by which a person might be healed. Instead, Step 4 prepares us to take Step 5 and to experience the much-needed sense of relief that it brings.

The 5th Step is when the writer of the inventory meets with an understanding individual to read and discuss his 4th Step work, preferably very soon after the inventory has been completed.[55]

There is an important spiritual principle that lies behind this uncomfortable divulging. The 5th Step states that we are to "admit to God, to ourselves, and to another human being the exact nature of our wrongs." The principle that *we cannot fully admit a thing to God unless we have admitted it to another person* may not be self-evident, but all who have tried this approach will attest to its truth.

Indeed, the humility involved in sharing our weakness with another person is invaluable. It helps us to feel unified with the human race and with God. People who have tried Step 5 often describe feeling like God has "heard them" in a fresh way. Since the relief and help are so beneficial, many will find themselves

---

[55] While it may take as little time to complete as one hour, in all likelihood it will require a longer session. A person might even schedule the 5th Step meeting before the inventory has been finished to give themselves a deadline. Saturday afternoons are perfect for a thorough 5th Step.

taking this step more than once. In fact, it sometimes becomes a way of life. The 5th Step teaches us a great lesson: *if you really want to bring God in on a particular situation, bring someone else in on it first.*

Notice another 5th Step principle: by confiding in another, we may be able to admit something to ourselves that we would not have otherwise been able to see. The listener will often share a bit of his own experience, or he will make a simple point that will come across to the person taking the 5th Step as a revelation.

Most people think they are unique, and in the 5th Step, they discover that they are not. Far from it, in fact. We think, "If anyone knew this about me, they would never talk to me again." The justifications for holding onto our secrets are the same things that cause us to feel irreconcilably separate from our fellow man.

The classic example described in many AA meetings concerns a person telling her sponsor in the 5th Step about "the worst thing I've ever done", to which the sponsor replies: "That's all? I did that twice!" In many cases, some terrible secret will elicit barely more than a raised eyebrow, or an, "uh-huh, what's next on your list?" from the sponsor. The unexceptional nature of most sin comes as a real surprise and relief to the person who takes the 5th Step honestly. In hearing a 5th Step, the sponsor should stress the reality that the sharer is indeed a member of the human race.

This is a sad truth, but a freeing one. I have almost never heard a male's 5th Step that has not involved some shameful sexual recollection. Most people have been involved in some kind of abuse. A big part of the healing that is needed in this area of life comes from finding out that "you're not the only one." If trust has been established with the listener, there is no reason why a tiny bit of questioning in this direction should be avoided; it may enable a person to experience an absolution of sorts that is equivalent to a massive amount of therapy. For this step, all that the listener needs is the ability to convey that what she is hearing is in no way exceptional, uncommon, or overly disconcerting.

In a rather serious sense, therapy and counseling are contemporary expressions of this confessional movement. A solitary life almost inevitably leads to a loss of perspective; people are simply not designed to live their lives on their own.[56] That is because we need each other, and furthermore, God often speaks through the mouths of other people. Seeking good counsel is what we might call "a no-brainer." For the alcoholic in search of sobriety, the 5th Step is vitally important, and a great many relapses have been attributed to people skipping it. As important as this step has been for AA, both modern psychotherapy and the Christian tradition also affirm the need for counseling and confession. This suggests the insight that *everyone could benefit from a 5th Step.*

The Big Book describes the wonderful feelings associated with completing the 5th Step in the following way:

> "Once we have taken this step, withholding nothing, we are delighted. We can look the world in the eye. We can be alone at perfect peace and ease. Our fears fall from us. We begin to feel the nearness of our Creator. We may have had certain spiritual beliefs, but now we begin to have a spiritual experience…We feel we are on the Broad Highway, walking hand in hand with the Spirit of the Universe" (75).

Confession in AA

"…in God's hands, the dark past is the greatest possession you have."
-*Big Book (24)*

---

[56] "Going it alone in spiritual matters is dangerous" (*12 & 12, 60*).

I once heard the story of a member of AA who was in need of a new sponsor. He needed to finish a 4th Step inventory that had been started a few months earlier with the help of a sponsor who had subsequently relapsed. Our friend was choosing a new sponsor based on who he thought had the most experience with the 5th Step. So he chose a famed old-timer who had heard countless 5th Steps and was known for his wisdom. Our friend described his excitement about getting to spend a prolonged period of time with this enlightened old fellow. He described his experience to me in the following way:

> "The actual experience of meeting with him on a Saturday afternoon to read my 4th Step turned out to be not at all what I expected. I had been expecting sage wisdom and insight into each of my particular resentments, as well as countless points that I had not considered before. Instead, he sat there across from me, listening in a seemingly detached fashion as I read to him.
>
> We both smoked a lot of cigarettes. He said 'next' a lot, sometimes even in the middle of my reading. It was like he didn't care or find any of my inventory to be very interesting. At one point, during the sex part, he divulged a very embarrassing story from his own past that put me right at ease. Other than that he said very little.
>
> The whole thing was done surprisingly quickly, sort of like the way an experienced doctor might visit with a patient in a hospital for only a very short period of time. All in all, the experience was remarkably unremarkable. It helped to redefine my understanding of both wisdom and spirituality. It taught me that being down-to-earth is more mystical than tripping on LSD!"

The 5th Step encounter benefits from a low-key vibe. It may take a little while to get the ball rolling, as the reader may wish to give her sponsor the context of a few of the first items on her list. Ideally, the sponsor should only be interested in the "my part" aspect. If the reader starts getting hung up on explaining the "why" behind the resentment, a good sponsor might cut them off sweetly, saying something like, "Thank you for helping me to better understand the situation. Now let's jump ahead to *your* part. What did you write down in answer to the questions I gave you?" In fact, two or three resentments deep into the inventory, it's a good idea to speed things up. Sponsors should be quick to acknowledge where the same material is being revisited: "Oh, it sounds a lot like the last one actually…"

Listeners generally see faults more easily than inventory-takers. The process, therefore, can be a matter of push-and-pull. At many points in the proceedings, it's up to the sponsor to hurry someone along. Sometimes, if I feel that we're covering redundant material, I'll abruptly cut off the reader with a slightly bored, "Next!" It's even okay to yawn while listening. At other times, however, I'll make them pause to dwell on something they are inclined to skim over.

Again, the listener's role is to help the subject see the running themes in his life that comprise his "character defects." You can write these on a piece of paper under the heading "Millie's Defects" or "Jason's Shortcomings", which will be given back to them at the end of your time together. Don't hesitate to ask them, "How would you describe that tendency in a word or two? I was thinking about writing: 'temper flare-ups.' Does that sound like a good way to describe this pattern we've seen three times in the past six resentments?"

At the end of the session, the listener reads the list of defects out loud and asks the inventory-taker if they think it's an accurate account of the negative character traits that have emerged in the process of reviewing the inventory. A recent list I compiled for a person included "road rage, social awkwardness, loneliness, difficulty separating work from the rest of my life, smoking, being cynical, lust, pushiness, shame about not finishing college." This list will be crucial for the next two steps.

The 5th Step is finished after someone has read his entire inventory to another person, sharing resentments, fears, and sexual history with the listener. At the end, there should be a list of character defects the sponsee can take home with them, a kind of summary of the problematic tendencies that have caused repeated trouble, discord, and unrest. If we don't have any defects, of course, then we won't be able to continue with the Twelve Steps.

Confession in Christianity

"Therefore confess your sins to each other and pray for each other so that you may be healed…"
-James 5:16

"Everyone who does evil hates the light, and will not come into the light for fear that their deeds will be exposed."
-John 3:20

The old-fashioned Christian word for Step 5 is "confession." This is simply the act of telling another person about one's sins, the ways in which our besetting weaknesses have manifested themselves concretely in our lives. A helpful Biblical description of this kind of ministry comes from the book of Hebrews, where the author writes that, "Every high priest [read: minister] is selected *from among the people* and is appointed to represent the people in matters related to God…He is able to deal gently with those who are ignorant and are going astray, since he himself is subject to weakness" (5:1-2).

The primary role of representing and serving God in ministry involves "dealing gently" with sinners, in light of the knowledge of one's own sin.

Few will contest that compassion for hardship is usually born of shared experience. Usually the person best suited to convey compassion to someone who has suffered a tragedy (e.g. miscarriage, cancer, or suicide) is the person who has experienced these things in their own life. The 5th Step represents a natural expression of this insight, and we see it clearly played out in the sponsor's bored "next –" following the most shameful confessions. This slight air of boredom conveys grace to the sponsee, letting him know that his sins are nothing exceptional in the community of sinners, and indeed that the sponsor has likely had firsthand experience with them.

Similarly, the sponsor might show great sensitivity over some small detail, or when the sponsee is noticeably reliving some traumatic memory from their past.[57] This too, is grace in practice. The Twelve Steps would suggest that being in touch with one's own past sinfulness and sufferings allows the hearer to show understanding. This facilitates the humble, forgiving attitude on the sponsor's part that helps confession accomplish its purpose: to be a tangible expression of God's one-way love, a word spoken into the individual's life that gives him certitude that he is indeed forgiven. The goal in confession is not to fix a person. It is to make the person feel understood, heard, and not condemned. The truth comes out and it is not held against them, but instead it is forgiven and absolved.

---

[57] If a deep sense of shame is connected to the material being discussed, I will try with my body language to convey that I am listening especially attentively, sometimes exhaling audibly.

AA's method operates implicitly upon the same theological principles that guide confession in the Church. The fact that confession works isn't due to some special status or deep spirituality in the hearer. Instead, we find confession's efficacy consists in *the concrete knowledge of forgiveness as it is extended to us in the specific context of our sins*. During the time of the Reformation, Martin Luther put forward the idea that every person who puts trust in God is, in turn, given a ministry on earth. The teaching came to be known as "the priesthood of all believers." In AA's 5th Step, the universal need for forgiveness aligns itself with the doctrine of "the priesthood of all believers" in a profound expression. This need reminds the Church that its calling to bring the Gospel message to life directly depends on how well it conveys forgiveness to its people.

Although confession's purpose in Christianity is to convey God's forgiveness and its corresponding freedom from guilt, it has a mixed history in the Church. Pop culture commonly portrays confession as something silly and archaic, something obligatory or, worse, a prison of guilt symbolized by a stifling confessional booth. Although the Church bears ultimate responsibility for these mixed messages, both Roman Catholic and Protestant churches have always believed that confession is not obligatory for forgiveness and, furthermore, that it is meant to convey grace. With all of this in view, confession is meant to be (and can be!) a reception of God's one-way love to us, distributed through another person. As FitzSimons Allison once remarked, "It's not something we *have* to do, it's something we *get* to do."

While we don't believe it's necessary in the traditional, whispering-sins-to-a-priest sort of way, AA's Step 5 highlights a useful practice for the Christian Church. Its honesty produces real results, corroborating the age-old truth that grace is an agent of change. Dietrich Bonhoeffer, the martyred German theologian, explained well confession's double-movement of the terror in having one's sin known and the grace that immediately follows from it:

> "You can hide nothing from God. The mask you wear before men will do no good before Him. He wants to see you as you are; He wants to be gracious to you. You do not have to go on lying to yourself and your brothers, as if you were without sin; you can dare to be a sinner. Thank God for that..."[58]

Because of confession's value, it's not surprising to find that corporate confession and absolution occur in every Sunday service in most denominations. In the church where I serve currently, each week we read the same Bible passage from the *Book of Common Prayer*, one which grasps the heart of the confessional dynamic. In simple terms, this verse offers the sense of peace that comes with completion of the 5th Step or with a healthy practice of Christian confession. We close with it:

"Come unto me all ye that travail and are heavy-laden, and I will refresh you."
-Matt 11:28

---

[58] Dietrich Bonhoeffer, *Life Together*, trans. John W. Doberstein (San Francisco: Harper & Row, 1954), 111.

Step 6

"Were Entirely Ready to Have God Remove These Defects of Character"

"The problem with a living sacrifice is that it keeps crawling off the altar."
-Unknown

"Character defect? My sponsor told me I'm a defect in search of some character."
-AA member working the 6th Step, South Carolina

Step 6 begins the moment we finish Step 5. That is, it begins once the reading of our moral inventory has yielded its list of undesirable character traits. Not surprisingly, the initial feeling of relief that comes from the 5th Step is soon replaced by the frustration that comes from trying to master character defects.

If you don't have a written list, it might be helpful to pause here to make a quick mental one. What aspects of your personality typically rub people the wrong way? Are you a picky eater, constantly giving waiters a bunch of extra instructions even though it makes your husband want to hide under the table? Are you a hypochondriac? Or a loud talker? Are you grumpy or impatient? Do have a temper with your family members?

Character defects are deeply-ingrained, unruly foes. One wise AA old-timer, Milt L. from Cleveland, compared them to "that game at Chuck E. Cheese":

> "You get the mallet in your hand and you start hitting those ugly puffy clowns as they pop up on that board with the six holes in it. You hit the thing over here and then a new one pops up over there. You hit that one, and then another one pops up in a different spot. Every time you hit the thing, a new thing pops up somewhere else."

The image is fitting. The battle with our defects is often defined by defeats in the same way that the story of alcoholism is often best understood by looking at relapses. Step 6 provides a concrete opportunity to reflect upon that list of defects and, if need be, add to it. Despite their persistence and unhealthiness , *our list of defects comprises our "spiritual resume." Indeed, to our way of thinking it is what qualifies us to build a strong relationship with God.*

Defects loom over our lives, and we sometimes find that our attempts to muzzle them provoke their re-emergence. St. Paul had a similar insight in his Letter to the Romans, where he writes, "Once I was alive apart from the law; but when the commandment came, sin sprang to life and I died" (7:9). The experience of trying to get better usually involves some aspect of disillusionment and regression.

Perhaps, during the 4th and 5th Step process, some things were revealed to us about our character that we had never consciously seen before. It is more likely, however, that we have been aware of the items on our lists for some time, but had never tried looking at them all together as a group. Not surprisingly, the 5th Step usually provokes a desire to be rid of the personality traits that have been defeating us in our day-to-day lives. Up until this point, we've justified or counter-balanced them against the weaknesses of others. Now, having focused entirely upon ourselves in the inventory, the (unsavory) fruit of that investigation sits before us.

The way that AA suggests we deal with our defects begins with the same type of moves we have found in the earlier steps: we look at the various ways we have failed to deal with them.

Absolutely Unable to Stop...on the Basis of Self-Knowledge (39)

"The presupposition that the will is able and willing to carry into effect what reason dictates is false."
-Karl Holl

"Knowing is half the battle."
-G. I. Joe

In Step 6, we are forced to re-evaluate our understanding of self-knowledge. Do you remember those instructional lessons that used to come at the very end of each episode of the 1980s children's cartoon *G.I. Joe*? They would show, for example, a hapless kid about to stick his finger in a socket. At the last possible instant one of the heroes from the series would show up to prevent the catastrophe. He would say something like, "Billy, don't stick your finger in electrical outlets or you'll get electrocuted." Then Billy would say, "Thanks for saving me. Now I know not to stick my fingers into electrical sockets," to which the G. I. Joe would respond, "And knowing is half the battle!" It was a slogan of sorts: "Knowing is half the battle." AA's philosophy looks upon this comment with amused skepticism. You can almost hear some wise old-timer in an AA meeting exclaim, *"Knowing may be half the battle... but it sure isn't the whole victory!"* as he slaps his knee.

To illustrate this point, consider the story of the watermelon farmer. He loved his watermelons and grew them with great affection. But he had one nagging problem: a group of "punk kids" were known from time to time to terrorize his beloved watermelon patch, usually stealing some of his best produce. Every year when the watermelons got large enough for harvest, these sneaky saboteurs would infiltrate his patch and make off with some of his crop.

The farmer tried all kinds of techniques to protect his watermelons. He would stay awake in his porch rocking chair, shotgun in his lap, waiting for the assailants. But they would show up just as he nodded off and be gone before he could even fire off a shot. His frustrations mounted from year to year until finally he built a fence around the patch. They still broke in. The next year he lined it with barbed-wire. He bought guard dogs and a security system. But all of these measures failed to prevent the surprisingly wily thieves from breaking in. His preoccupation with security grew into a perennial source of anxiety and neurosis.

Finally one night, just before the new crop reached harvest time, the farmer came up with a brilliant plan to stop the thieves. He woke up early the next morning, went into his shed and created a small sign, which he attached to a stake. He planted it right in the middle of the patch. It read: *"One of these watermelons is poisoned."* Finally, for the first time in weeks, he slept well, knowing that the thieves would stay away for fear of being poisoned.

The next morning he walked out to the watermelon patch with an air of confidence. His smile was quickly replaced by a frown when he noticed something written on his sign. The word "one" had been crossed out with a black slash. Scrawled just above it was the word "two", so that the sign now read: *"Two of these watermelons are poisoned."*

The point is that, as far as Step 6 is concerned, our best thinking and planning is not enough to beat our defects of character. We cannot change ourselves, even if we understand the ways in which we would like to change. Shel Silverstein points this out in his classic poem, "The Little Blue Engine": "If the track is tough and the hill is rough, THINKING you can just ain't enough." Until we view our inflexible personalities this way, we will remain stuck in our delusions about both ourselves and the world at large.

Likewise, in the religious realm, churches that fail to account for the realities of recidivism – or the tendency to fall back into reprehensible behavior – in the life of Christians have a hard time connecting with their congregations over the long haul. Lutheran theologian Steven Paulson has noted the "vast difference it makes for a preacher to stand before a congregation and assume their wills are bound rather than to stand before a group and assume their wills are merely in need of motivation."[59]

Theologian Rod Rosenbladt captures the 6th Step bind as it often presents itself in the mind of a Christian in his pamphlet *Christ Alone:*

> "Think of the inner soliloquy many Christians experience week by week: 'There may have been grace for me when, as a sinner, I was initially converted. But now, having been given the Spirit of God, I fear that things have gotten worse in me rather than better. I

---

[59] Stephen Paulson, introduction to *The Captivation of the Will: Luther vs. Erasmus on Freedom and Bondage*, by Gerhard O. Forde (Grand Rapids, MI: Eerdmans, 2005), xi.

have horribly abused all of God's good gifts to me. I was so optimistic in the beginning, when the pastor told me that Christ outside of me, dying for me, freely saved me by his death, and that the Holy Spirit now dwelling within me would aid me in following Christ…I have rededicated myself to Christ more times than I can count. But it seems to stay the same, or even get worse, no matter what I do. Whatever the outer limits of Christ's grace are, I have certainly crossed them. I have utterly, consciously, and with planning aforethought blown it all.

"'I guess I was never a Christian in the first place, because if I had been, I would have made some progress in the Christian life…I'll try going to church for a while longer, but I think I've tried every possible thing the church has told me to do. After that, I guess I'll return to paganism and 'eat, drink, and be merry' for the time I've got left. What else is there to do?'"[60]

Rosenbladt's quote perfectly depicts the psychological state that accompanies the experience of the 6th Step for people in AA. While some may hope that working the steps will quickly change them in an easily discernible way, the reality of the spiritual life does involve frequent disappointment – and this disappointment has a profundity and transformative power all its own.

Think about your most glaring defects for a moment. Have you been able to rid yourself of them? What would your closest friends say? Can you identify with the train of thought described in Rosenbladt's soliloquy? For example, are you a smoker? Smoking is a perfect example of a character defect. It's unhealthy and hard to defend. Yet tons of people do it; they love smoking, but they

---

[60] Rod Rosenbladt, *Christ Alone*, (Wheaton, IL: Crossway Books, 1999), 39-40.

hate being smokers. Most smokers want to quit, at least theoretically. But "quitting time" never seems to arrive or, for that matter, it never seems to last very long when it does arrive.

Step 6 requires us to look our defects square in the face. How much of your life has been defined by your defects? How many attempts have you made to beat them? What's the longest you've had a defect lie dormant? If you beat it, did two or three new ones arrive in its place? And are they still with you?

If we're to understand what Step 6 means when it says "were entirely ready to have God remove our defects of character", we will need to address the fact that *self-knowledge, in and of itself, does not provide the means necessary to defeat defects*. George Eliot captures this perfectly in her short story *Janet's Repentance*:

> "She was tired, she was sick of that barren exhortation — Do right, and keep a clear conscience, and God will reward you, and your troubles will be easier to bear. She wanted strength to do right — she wanted something to rely on besides her own resolutions; for was not the path behind her all strewn with broken resolutions? How could she trust in new ones?"[61]

Self-knowledge, without the aid of outside power, does little more than laugh at our failures. Unflinching honesty produces despair rather than hope. Step 6 understands that the state of continual relapse is common in human nature, and that we need more than simple self-knowledge to re-habituate the individual's will. This is an understanding that is just as important for the church to recover as it is for alcoholics.

---

[61] George Eliot, *Scenes of Clerical Life* (New York, NY: Oxford UP, 1988), 252

"Were Entirely Ready" and the Defense That Precedes Readiness

"The only wisdom we can hope to acquire is the wisdom of humility: humility is endless."
-T.S. Eliot

"When the ground crumbles under their feet, [people] have to leap even into uncertainty if they are to avoid certain destruction."
-W. H. Auden

People are quick to make excuses for themselves. We defend our defects of character on the grounds that we cannot change them. They come with us; they are part of the package. Maybe you've met a person who says of themselves, "I'm a control freak, so…" or, "I don't like surprises" or, "I'm a big talker." To some extent, they are describing defects that have taken over their lives, defects that define their self-understanding. Indeed, our defects can make us think of ourselves as a closed system. If our "system" cannot eradicate them, then it incorporates them and defends their presence.

Step 6 acknowledges the presence of our defects and their deep-seated, barnacle-like attachment to us. But it also refuses to excuse them, in spite of the fact that they have not yielded to the headlong assault of the will. If certain patterns of behavior and thinking have caused us to harm ourselves, our neighbors, or our relationship with God, AA would suggest that we view them through a critical lens.

This means that the defects on our list can be things that we both like *and* dislike. While we may be understandably reluctant to criticize the things about ourselves that we hold dear, if they are the same qualities that create distance between us and our fellow man (and God), they need to come under scrutiny. Inventory has opened the door to the idea that we may, in fact, need a complete make-over and not just a little bit of tweaking. In this way, we begin to view our lives from God's perspective rather than from the vantage point of our own navels. Again, the formal religious word for this is "repentance." Indeed, the 6th Step dynamic is so central to spirituality that Martin Luther believed that the whole life of believers should be characterized as one of repentance.

Step 6 involves looking at the various ways we have defended and justified our shortcomings. In many instances we actually find that we love our character defects. We don't want to be rid of them, and we definitely don't want to know what life would be like without them. A perfect example of this comes from a column Mark Oppenheimer wrote for Slate in 2011 entitled "The Unholy Pleasure: My Life-Long Recovery from Snobbery." We quote from it at some length because he makes the point so well:

> "It is not unusual for snobberies to begin as self-defense—they are almost necessarily the province of minority groups worried that they might any day be vanquished: The landed English were surrounded by the peasants, the educated Ivy Leaguers by *hoi polloi*. Beneath the airs of superiority one can quickly discern the grounding of insecurity…
>
> "But self-protective armor can be used in the offensive, too; judgment nearly always turns judgmental. Nobody likes to relinquish a snobbery, even when it becomes safe to venture forth without it… Wherever snobbery can be found, it is evidence of insecurity, even emotional poverty; and yet it is frequently one of life's great pleasures…
>
> "The problem, of course, is that after a while the snobbery game, like any game played consistently over

many years, becomes quite serious. Just as there are no true "recreational" golfers, there is after a while no such thing as a recreational snob. The judgmentalism moves to the fore, and the snob really begins to see people as mere butterflies, objects for classification... Snobbery is ultimately a dysfunction.

"...I do wonder if I can ever change; I cannot decide if I even want to."[62]

Here we see the flipside of our personalities. We are defect-laden people, and yet imagining ourselves without our defects is almost impossible. This becomes especially clear when we understand that even our favorite things about ourselves (e.g. where we went to school, or our community-service track record, or our career success) can be the biggest hindrances to our spiritual lives. It's a great and important point and one that the New Testament frequently makes – that self-righteousness is more detrimental to the maintenance of a relationship with God than despair and humility.[63]

I'm in a 6th Step State of Mind

In order to better make sense of the 6th Step state of mind, let's consider its opposite for moment. A few years ago, a young professional named John Fitzgerald Page made headlines when a young woman, who had approached him on Match.com,

---

[62] Mark Oppenheimer, "The Unholy Pleasure: My Life-Long Recovery from Snobbery", *Slate*, January 24, 2011, http://www.slate.com/.
[63] For New Testament examples of this, see the older brother in the Parable of the Prodigal Son (Lk 15:11-32), the story of the Pharisee and the tax collector (Lk 18:9-14), or the Parable of the Workers in the Vineyard (Mt. 20:1-16).

published two of his emails to her. Here's the report the girl wrote:[64]

> "So I winked at this guy on Match. Should have known better considering his screen name was 'IvyLeagueAlum.' He responds with the following email...
>
> "I live in a 31 story high rise condominium, right in the middle of the Buckhead nightlife district. Do you ever come to this area of town to shop/go out/visit/ explore?
>
> I went to an Ivy League school - the University of Pennsylvania - for my undergraduate degree in economics and my graduate degree in management (Wharton School of Business). Where did you go to school?
>
> What activities do you currently participate in to stay in shape? I work out 4 times a week at LA Fitness. Do you exercise regularly? I am 6 feet tall, 185 pounds - what about yourself? I am truly sorry if that sounds rude, impolite or even downright crass, but I have been deceived before by inaccurate representations so I prefer someone be upfront and honest on initial contact...
>
> I do mergers & acquisitions (corporate finance) for Limited Brands (Bath & Body Works, Victoria's Secret, etc). Enjoy any of our stores/divisions?
>
> Do you have any other recent pictures you care to share? I have many others if you care to see them.
>
> -Regards, John"

---

[64] Emily Gould, "Nightmare Online Dater John Fitzgerald Page Is the Worst Person in the World", *Gawker*, October 7, 2011, http://www.gawker.com/.

"So I in turn send him a polite 'No Thanks' thru the Match system which sends him the following email: 'Thanks for writing to me, but unfortunately, we're just not a good match. Good luck in your search! Our Portraits didn't match on: A. Personality.'"

John then responded with the following email:

"I think you forgot how this works. You hit on me, and therefore have to impress ME and pass MY criteria and standards - not vice versa. 6 pictures of just your head and your inability to answer a simple question lets me know one thing. You are not in shape. I am a trainer on the side, in fact, I am heading to the gym in 26 minutes!

So next time you meet a guy of my caliber, instead of trying to turn it around, just get to the gym! I will even give you one free training session, so you don't blow it with the next 8.9 on Hot or Not, Ivy League grad, Mensa member, can bench/squat/leg press over 1200 lbs., has had lunch with the secretary of defense, has an MBA from the top school in the country, lives in a Buckhead high rise, drives a Beemer convertible, has been in 14 major motion pictures, was in Jezebel's Best dressed, etc. Oh, that is right, there aren't any more of those!

-Regards, John"

Like all of us, poor John is rife with character defects. We could easily list the ones he forgets to mention, but the example reveals just how, in God's world, a strength can be a weakness.

The Big Book is quick to point out this twist, that we tend to gravitate toward – rather than away from – our defects, thinking that they are strengths. The 6th Step prayer spells it out beautifully:

"If we still cling to something we will not let go, we ask God to help us be willing" (77). It is partly for this reason that the 7th Step will ask us to pray that God will take *both* "the good and the bad" that exists within us, for the "good" may in fact be our bad.

Hopefully it has become clear that the phrase "were entirely ready" actually means: "were entirely miserable about the person we have become, and also about our inability or lack of desire to change ourselves." Step 6 is the place where we see ourselves continuing to exhibit the qualities that we most dislike about ourselves. And it is also the place where we recognize that we like the things about ourselves that we should find most repulsive. Step 6 is the brick wall against which we bang our head, and it is the claw marks on the things about ourselves that we are hanging onto. Step 6 is honest frustration and undefended vulnerability.

Step 6 is, in some sense, a continuation of Step 1. Once people realize that their lives have become unmanageable because of their fundamentally impaired selves, it then makes sense to examine selfishness more closely in Step 4 and then, digging deeper in Step 5, to examine particular character defects. The honesty of Step 6 concerning one's shortcomings also makes a great deal of sense in Christianity, which describes all people as sinful and locates their fundamental problem in pride.

The Defect of Self-Justification

One fundamental expression of our character defects is the universal phenomenon of self-justification. Self-justification is simply our bias towards believing we act rightly, even when our actions are destructive, hurtful, or in some other way at cross-purposes with the best interests of ourselves and others. In a social science book called *Mistakes Were Made (But Not by Me)*, two authors explore this universal human desire to justify our actions:

> "We look at the behavior of politicians with amusement or alarm or horror, but, psychologically, what they do is no different…from what most of us have done at one time or another in our private lives. We stay in an unhappy relationship or merely one that is going nowhere because, after all, we invested so much time in making it work. We stay in a deadening job way too long because we look for all the reasons to justify staying and are unable to clearly assess the benefits of leaving. We buy a lemon of a car because it looks gorgeous, spend thousands of dollars to keep the damn thing running, and then we spend even more to justify that investment…"[65]

We have a natural inclination to view our actions and choices as good and right and valuable, even if they are quite the opposite, and the result is self-justification. If we offend someone, we assume it is they who are too sensitive; if someone criticizes us, we deflect it by classifying them as a nitpicky person who doesn't know us that well anyway. It is no surprise that in most marriages, each spouse thinks that he or she bears a greater load of household chores than they actually do. We overestimate our contributions and underestimate our faults, and yet the nagging feelings of guilt and failure still don't go away. Steps 1-6 are intended to give us a more honest view of ourselves than we will ever receive from the inner voice of self-justification.

---

[65] Carol Tavris and Elliot Aronson, *Mistakes Were Made (but not by me): Why We Justify Foolish Beliefs, Bads Decisions, and Hurtful Acts* (Orlando, FL: Harcourt, 2007).

In Christianity, this rigorous assessment of ourselves is often described in terms like original sin, total depravity, or the ongoing power of the flesh (Gal. 5:16-21) and the 'old man' in human lives (Rom. 6:6; Col. 3;9). Rightly diagnosing self-justification as connected to pride, lack of self-honesty, and refusal to recognize one's need for God, the Protestant Reformers viewed human reliance on ourselves and our own powers as a critical problem.

It is a tragic fact that the Christian church has so often been guilty of just this sort of un-self-aware self-justification, and corresponding self-righteousness, arrogance, judgmentalism, and condescension towards others. The accusations of hypocrisy frequently leveled against the church for seeing the speck in the eyes of others but not recognizing the log in its own are in many instances difficult to refute. Religious self-justification finds especially fertile ground in the belief that believers are special or more morally sound people than non-Christians.

In light of this recurrent problem in the church, it is striking to recognize that at the core of Christianity is an idea that demolishes such hypocrisy and targets the deceit of self-justification like a heat-seeking missile. In the 16th century, a monk named Martin Luther read the New Testament with fresh eyes and in light of his own religious strivings and failures and saw there an idea often called "justification by faith." Justification by faith is the understanding that God finds human beings acceptable and lovable not because of who they are or what they have done, but because of who He is and what He has done. In this understanding, Christian faith is the belief that God saves and rescues us precisely in our failures, our needs, and the inescapability of our character defects. In the Anglican *Book of Common Prayer*, God's attitude towards human beings is described in a two-fold manner: "Not weighing our merits, but pardoning our offenses." In other words, the thrust of justification by faith is two-fold: we are not righteous by our own merits, but neither are we penalized for our sin.

The idea of justification by faith, like Step 6, thus encourages us to look honestly at our character defects, because it is there that God greets us with mercy and compassion. He doesn't accept us because we do good; rather, it is our very sinfulness and limitation that drives us to Him. Since we have no righteousness to bring us to God, He must use our wrongdoing to bring us to Him. For the Church to address its problems of hypocrisy and judgmentalism, an excellent place to start would be a return to this core Christian idea of justification by faith. By recovering this idea, the Church could at the same time begin to retrieve a rigorous, Step 6-style honesty about human limitations, as well as an understanding that such honesty has its own transformative power.

The Protestant Reformer Thomas Cranmer constructed a series of prayers known as "collects" which accompany the Christian Church calendar and are read at each service from the *Book of Common Prayer*. One of the most beautiful prayers from that collection is the "Collect for the First Sunday after Epiphany." In it Cranmer draws attention to two primary aspects of life: first, that we need to see things rightly (which, in the case of the self, is "half the battle"); and second, that we have no power over our shortcomings without external help. The latter is the subject of the next step, Step 7, and Cranmer's words prepare the way:

> *"Lord, we beseech thee mercifully to receive the prayers of thy people which call upon thee; and grant that they may both perceive and know what things they ought to do, and also have grace and power faithfully to fulfill the same."*

Step 7

"Humbly Asked Him to Remove Our Shortcomings"

"Only the saint knows sin."
-William Porcher Dubose

None of the Twelve Steps exist in a vacuum. In the same way that Step 2 naturally precedes Step 3, and that there cannot be a 5th Step unless a 4th Step inventory has been written, so it is with Step 7, which is crucially dependent upon Step 6. In fact, no two steps are as interrelated as Steps 6 & 7. Without a knowledge of one's shortcomings, there can be no genuine impetus to ask God to remove them.

These steps are so closely linked that the Big Book deals with them in almost the same breath, in a notoriously short two-paragraph passage. It is all that is written in the text about these two somewhat mysterious steps. For this reason, Steps 6 & 7 are sometimes called "the forgotten steps." But much can be said about them.

Asking for Help

At the core of Step 7 lies a prayer:

> "My Creator, I am now willing that you should have all of me, good and bad. I pray that you now remove from me every single defect of character which stands in the way of my usefulness to you and my fellows. Grant me strength, as I go out from here, to do your bidding. Amen." (76)

The prayer voices a request to God for help with "every single defect of character which stands in the way of my usefulness to you and my fellows." Indeed, it asks for their "removal." The idea implicit in Step 7 is that people, in and of themselves, are incapable of beating or removing their defects on their own. Help is needed. In the case of the sad-sap alcoholic, the reception of divine help is obviously equivalent to an experience of grace, for it is not deserved and yet it is given.

You and I are typically reluctant to ask for help. In fact, we often reject help even when it is offered. The TV drama *Breaking Bad*, for example, tells the story of a man named Walter White, who would rather become a drug dealer than accept help in paying for his chemotherapy. Walter White's reluctance is extreme, but it is not uncommon. People typically wish to avoid any suggestion that they are not the primary solution to their problems. Alcoholics Anonymous would wholly disagree with the well-meaning new age saying that "the answer is within you."

Step 7 sees the desire to ask for help as a great spiritual breakthrough. This insight was discussed at length in Step 3, but Step 7 applies it to a concrete series of issues. It is where we learn to pray in the most practical sense for God's help with life. Step 7 asks God to be the one who will solve our problems.

Praying the List

"I'm at my most victorious when I'm on my knees."
-Unknown

What does this look like in practice? In the most straightforward sense, Step 7 simply involves praying on a daily basis for God to remove our defects of character. Personally, I perform Step 7 with the help of two bits of text. The first is the 7th Step prayer quoted above, and the second is the list of defects I got from Step 6.

In the earliest days of AA, Step 7 had a tiny phrase added to it. While it now reads: "Humbly asked Him to remove our shortcomings", the step originally read: "Humbly *on our knees* asked Him to remove our shortcomings." The "on our knees" part is obviously not crucial, but perhaps it gives us a picture of the humility that true prayer naturally invites. We kneel so that God might stand in our place.

Taking my copy of the Big Book and my list of defects in hand, I hit my knees at the foot of my bed. Then I say the 7th Step prayer–I say it aloud, but silently works well, too—exactly as it is written. When I get to the part that says, *"My Creator, I am now willing that you should have all of me, good and bad. I pray that you now remove from me every single defect of character which stands in the way of my usefulness to you and my fellows,"* I pause and turn my attention to my list of shortcomings, reciting them in the order they are written, in the same way that I might read off of a grocery list, only with a bit more attention so that I feel like I mean what I'm saying.[66] For example, "my temper, my lust, my being overly talkative, my inability to keep secrets, my smoking, my social awkwardness, my poor eating habits." I then I finish the prayer: *"Grant me strength, as I go out from here, to do your bidding. Amen,"* after which I get up and begin my day.[67]

How Does God Answer a (7th Step) Prayer?

"When I am weak, then I am strong."
-2 Corinthians 12:10

"Only he can see his sin who has the Holy Spirit."
-Bo Giertz

In order to best appreciate the ways in which people change as a result of Step 7, it is helpful to consider the ways in which the 7th Step prayer is typically *not* answered. I have yet to meet a person who says that, once they started praying about their defects, they were all removed instantly and forever.

No one ever graduates from needing God's help. The reality of the spiritual life is that *need-for-God grows, it does not diminish*. As a consequence, people who pray for God to remove their character defects rarely find that they are removed in an obvious fashion; that is, the removal of defects is usually not very evident to the person praying for their removal.

---

[66] A brief tangent: although some AAs have wished to draw a distinction between the "defects of character" of Step 6 with the "shortcomings" of Step 7, Bill W. was quick to offer a corrective on this matter. He said that he was taught that "good writers don't use the same words over and over", so in Step 7 he used a different word, "shortcomings", in place of "defects of character." They are the same thing.

[67] Later, in Steps 10 & 11, we will see how this simple minute-long practice can be incorporated into a more developed devotional time.

In the Sermon on the Mount, Jesus' offers a pertinent image of a right hand not being aware of what a left hand is doing (Mt. 6:3). Usually, the person who prays for God's help is slow to see its appearance. One reason for this is that once a person's life belongs to God, their improvements occur for the sake of others and not for the self-centered benefit of the individual. That the individual appreciates the removal of defects is almost an afterthought.

Spirituality is not about growing in self-improvement, but about growing in usefulness to God. As the Big Book reminds us, "Our real purpose is to fit ourselves to be of maximum service to God and the people about us" (77). In Step 7 we realize that our problems are primarily detrimental to us because of the way they hinder our usefulness to other people, not because of the discomfort they create for us. In effect, the world benefits from our 7th Step work more than we do.[68]

Step 7 involves laying our problematic tendencies prayerfully before God and then trusting Him to work on them in whatever way He deems fit. We trust His judgment about what we need over and above our own. We lay our life before God in all its ugliness, and we then proceed with our day, hoping against hope that we will not get in the way of the opportunities we are given to share God's love with the world.

---

[68] The goal of personal improvement is perhaps best pursued by joining a gym or some form of new-age practice that focuses on becoming "the person you want to be." Step 7 is about becoming the person God wants you to be. Chances are, those two people are very different versions of you.

Getting Worse Is Getting Better?

"Although people do sometimes have a sense of peace with God...nevertheless, in a given situation it is not so much peace with God that is the true mark of the Holy Spirit at work, but birth pangs."
-Christoph Blumhardt

Another image of God's work in a person's life comes from John's Gospel: "The wind blows wherever it pleases. You hear its sound, but you cannot tell where it comes from or where it is going. So it is with everyone born of the Spirit" (3:8). During the 7th Step, defects can often seem to get worse, as though God's power is blowing fickly from one random branch of our lives to the next.

On some days there seems to be very little wind. On other days things are gusty and inconsistent. Occasionally, the feeling of God's presence in the midst of problematic situations is almost overwhelming. In each case, the individual has very little control over how it goes. Good sponsors consequently tend to encourage their sponsees to practice the 7th Step relentlessly for at least a month or two without forming any judgment on whether or not it's "working." You can imagine that a sapling, if it is dug up every day to check for root growth, will have a much harder time growing than one that is simply watered, exposed to sunlight, and left alone.

Why wouldn't God remove defects in a way that is easily measurable to the recipient? A few reasons: First, it teaches us to rely upon God and not upon ourselves. Second, we must question the level of insight we have into our lives. Few people see themselves accurately, alcoholic or not. For people in a romantic relationship, for example, a significant other usually recognizes 7th Step changes first. Third, it draws our focus away from the areas where God is, in fact, improving things in us. True changes sometimes happen slowly and are difficult for us to recognize. This allows us to remain prayerful and focused on the only place where true solutions are found. While we're preoccupied with one part of life, God is usually at work in another area, unbeknownst to us.

Fourth, it often feels like things are getting worse because we are starting to view our lives by a new set of incredibly stringent standards – not necessarily because we actually are getting worse. As C. S. Lewis once commented, "The closer you get to the sun, the bigger the shadow." An AA doing the 7th Step has begun to view her life from God's perspective, rather than her own. The old life is no longer easily justified. Nor is it defended. If nothing else, entering into this mindset brings about a fresh measure of humility. As Chuck T. used to say: "The thing about meekness [which is good] and weakness [which we think is bad] is that *they feel the same.*"

Finally, a person who is praying for God to remove his shortcomings might not be able to detect any answer because a new approach to life is being developed in them. This has more to do with praying than with having prayers answered. In many important respects, the prayer itself is the answer to the shortcoming. Our self-reliance is eroding and continual reliance upon God is taking its place. It's actually the most wonderful thing in the world!

In my own experience, I remember being incredibly frustrated by the 7th Step and God's failure to answer my prayers in a lasting fashion. I remember exaggerating stories and dishonestly embellishing in my conversations with friends, for example. Then I would awkwardly apologize, correcting the details in the middle of re-telling a story.

After the conversation was over, I would run through the series of events in my head, praying, "God, forgive me for being dishonest, and please remove my dishonesty." And then, seemingly five minutes later, I would find myself doing the same thing again. If I was not repeating the lying, like our earlier whack-a-mole analogy, I would be thinking some incredibly judgmental thought about another person in place of the still-smarting lie. This went on for weeks and months, and my alone time, walking to and from the subway, was riddled with endless self-criticism and confused attempts at 7th Step prayer. After a few months of this, I called my father, who is a minister and – to my way of thinking – a very spiritual man.

I burst out, "Dad, I must be doing something wrong. I pray for God to forgive me and to help me not do whatever it is I've just done again…and then five minutes later, I do it again. I'm trapped in this cycle and I honestly feel like I'm going insane!" After a brief pause, my father replied, "*Son… welcome to the Christian life.*"

An important part of Step 7 is acknowledging the fact that a person never graduates from the need for dependence upon God's grace in the midst of life's difficulties. St. Paul famously described this dynamic at the end of his Second Letter to the Corinthian Church. He recounted having a "thorn in the flesh," which he repeatedly prayed for God to remove. God did no such thing, and for this, Paul later came to be incredibly grateful. He writes:

> "In order to keep me from becoming conceited, I was given a thorn in my flesh, a messenger of Satan, to torment me. Three times I pleaded with the Lord to take it away from me. But he said to me, 'My grace is sufficient for you, for my power is made perfect in weakness.' Therefore I will boast all the more gladly about my weaknesses, so that Christ's power may rest on me. That is why, for Christ's sake, I delight in

weaknesses, in insults, in hardships, in persecutions, in difficulties. For when I am weak, then I am strong."
(2 Cor 12: 7-10)

AA on Sanctification: Still Bob, Still Sober, or *Simul Iustus Et Peccator*

In the Christian faith, the term "sanctification" refers to the way in which God's grace transforms an individual life. It is a topic that has divided Christians for centuries. AA has become a contemporary think tank on the question, and it has some valuable contributions to offer the Church.

In spite of newfound sobriety, the sober alcoholic still struggles with the same powerlessness that afflicted him in the midst of his drinking. Many Christians would instead claim that once a person establishes a relationship with a saving God, they become measurably empowered to fend off temptation and self-centeredness through the indwelling of the Holy Spirit. AA would look upon this claim with skepticism, as one adage demonstrates: "Once a pickle, you can't go back to being a cucumber, even if you're no longer sitting in a jar of pickle juice." In other words: once an alcoholic, always an alcoholic. As one gentleman observed, "I thought when I got sober that I was no longer going to be Bob, but guess what? I'm still Bob, even though I'm sober."

God's transformative work in the life of a sober alcoholic has more to do with perspective and faith than with ontological alteration. In more strictly religious terms, sinners remain sinful even after they find salvation. The empirical evidence in support of this claim is overwhelming, though its implications are somewhat disappointing for the struggler who hopes all will be well once her life is placed in God's care.

In contrast to this sort of spiritual idealism, Bob's earlier statement reflects an incredibly important insight that emerged in the 16th century during the Protestant Reformation. We again reference Luther's insight that a spiritual person is "simultaneously justified and fallen."

Martin Luther believed that the Christian stands before God completely exonerated of all guilt, treated as though his or her life is as righteous as Christ's own perfect one. The word for this gracious covering-up of our guilt before God is "justification." In spite of the fact that we are justified, humans in and of ourselves still struggle in the same ways we did before finding faith. In other words, a spiritual person is simultaneously Saint (from God's vantage point) *and* Sinner (from a human vantage point). Rather than being either good *or* bad, the Christian is viewed as both good *and* bad in the same moment.[69] In contrast to so much modern Christian self-understanding, the Protestant Reformation affirmed that God operates primarily outside of and upon humans, rather than in or alongside them.

An AA known as "Happy Jack" once told the following story about himself:

> "Last week I got a resentment at my wife because she decided to file for divorce on the one year anniversary of my mother's death. So I was angry at her, to say the least. But I did what I've always been told to do in AA whenever I'm angry: I went to a meeting, and you know what? It didn't help …although it did. Then I helped out a new guy in the group who was having a rough time, and you know what? It didn't help …although it did. Then I called my sponsor and told him about the resentment, and he asked me what my part was in all of

---

[69] To quote AA's *7th Step Prayer:* "My Creator, I am now willing that you should have all of me, good and bad."

it, and you know what? That didn't help either
…although it did."

As this example reveals, Luther's *simul iustus et peccator* describes even our daily emotional lives, with the tension between our failure to work for ourselves and God's work upon us. This dynamic is bandied about unwittingly in the rooms of AA.

When an alcoholic turns her life over to God in Step 3, she has made a permanent, life-altering covenant with God that will have inexorable pull on her life from that moment until death. This implies that once God begins a work in the life of a person, that person is incapable of resisting His overarching sovereignty, even if she kicks and screams and does terrible things.[70] Another priceless AA adage puts it this way: "If you give your lunch to a gorilla, you don't get it back." Our ability to impact the world in a negative way becomes subsumed and superseded by the work that God intends for our lives.

There is immense freedom in this picture of life: God is actively at work in human life for His greater good, even when we cannot clearly see or understand how or where He is at work. The things of life that seem trivial, meaningless, or even terrible may still be the channels through which God is bringing about His glory.[71] We still feel the same, and yet we know by faith that all has changed. We see "through a glass darkly" as the New Testament puts it (1 Cor 13:12).

The ability to control God is completely written out of this equation. As one AA said to another, "Son, your life ain't none of your damn business!" Faith and total abandonment to God go

---

[70] This idea greatly resembles what, in Reformation terms, is known as "irresistible grace."
[71] In the Lutheran tradition, this understanding of spirituality is known as a "theology of the cross." For more on this, see Gerhard O. Forde, *On Being a Theologian of the Cross: Reflections on Luther's Heidelberg Disputation, 1518*.

hand in hand in AA. A life must be lost if it is ever to be found (Mt 16:25).

Defects Removed

"Of course, the often disputed question of whether God can – and will, under certain conditions – remove defects of character will be answered with a prompt affirmative by almost any AA member."
-12&12 (63)

In a general sense, God addresses our defects in two ways. In the first way, He works *in spite* of the continuing presence of our defects. In the second, He removes them in a more straightforward fashion. Let's look at both.

Type 1: Defects Removed? No, but Yes.

An important part of parenting comes when the parent makes a mistake. Perhaps tempers flare in a regrettable way. Or maybe a crucial decision turns out to have been a misstep. Maybe the parents move their child into a new school that proves to be a poor match, and the child has to switch back later. God's grace is often most palpable where good things happen in the wake of our mistakes. To revisit our earlier example, perhaps the child had such a terrible experience in the new school that, after an awful year there, he switches back and has a newfound appreciation for the old school, so much so that he begins to study more and loves his experience more than ever. These are the experiences of God's providence that make life in the midst of uncertainty bearable rather than paralyzing. If we make a mistake, God can right it or even undo it, sometimes bringing ultimate good out of our worst decisions. God redeems our lives because it is in His nature to do so. We do not have to live in fear that our life hangs in the balance of whether or not we make a "wrong move."[72]

The spiritual life that is lived on the other side of a mistake is more important than the life lived before it. The mistake provides the opportunity to fall into God's care, where we see just how big and powerful His goodness is. Often it is there that we find freedom. Such freedom is a spiritual gift, and the 7th Step opens the door to it. Indeed, much of the spiritual life described in the Twelve Steps involves living in the face of mistakes, as opposed to living rightly in order to avoid them. Wherever our steps fall, whether they are "on the path" or "off the beam", God is overarchingly present and working for good.

We may make a mistake or series of mistakes that leads to total collapse. God may allow a defect to persist toward exactly this end. Like the "Coffee with Jesus" cartoon above suggests, God may reply to our desire for easy, tangible results in the following manner: "I totally hear you. It's just that Carl's got some more falling to do before I can be of much help...It all works out in the end...the comeback is sweeter that way."[73] Where the

---

[72] Paul echoes this sentiment famously: "And we know that in all things God works for the good of those who love him, who have been called according to his purpose" (Rm 8:28).
[73] Used by permission of Radio Free Babylon, which is not affiliated with this book, its content, or Mockingbird.

shortcomings are not removed, the opportunity for a profoundly redemptive narrative only deepens. Imagine how different the Parable of the Prodigal Son would be if the prodigal son had gotten his life in order, found a steady job, and acquired a good reputation before returning to his father. The story would still have a happy ending, and yet it would not say as much about the depth of God's forgiveness – nor resonate as powerfully with our lived experience. The possibility of profound forgiveness becomes more concrete when the trespass is great. To quote Jesus' actual words, "Whoever has been forgiven little, loves little" (Lk 7:47).

Where a defect is not removed and unpalatable consequences ensue, we can faithfully affirm our hope of deliverance. One example of this counterintuitive turn of events comes in the famous story of Jacob in the Old Testament. Jacob spends a night wrestling with God. During one point in their struggle, God "touched the socket of Jacob's hip so that his hip was dislocated as he wrestled with the man" (Gen 32:25). Perhaps the dislocated hip, like the thorn in Paul's flesh, is something that provides the fuel for a much more significant fire later.

In a more overtly positive light, the assurance of God's work delivers us from a world of second-guessing and trouble-shooting, which are exactly the things we abandoned to God in the 3rd Step. Consider the following story of how one AA member came to appreciate this new perspective:

Stanley was a wise and well-regarded member of AA. He sponsored many people and was sought by many for his wise counsel. But Stanley was also a human being, still dealing his own defects of character. One afternoon, Stanley went for a jog, which was something he often did to clear his mind. On this one afternoon, things took a terrible turn when he tripped over a low-lying barbed wire fence that was wrapped around the base of a large tree. He hadn't seen it until it was too late.

Suddenly he was on the ground, and his right ankle was torn up in a few spots, not to mention the scrapes, bruises, and embarrassment. Stanley was also a bit of a vain fellow, and that "vanity" was indeed one of the shortcomings that he had been praying for God to remove from his life. As Stanley describes it, not only was he bleeding and in need of a few band-aids, but he was also livid. As he made his way home, he thought about how he could sue the person who had put the fence there. "The audacity!..." His mood had turned incredibly sour, far from the "serene and spiritual" demeanor for which he was known.

To top things off, he had already made plans to meet with two sponsees on either side of an AA meeting later that evening. Begrudgingly, Stanley still made it to the coffee shop where he met up with Sponsee #1. In spite of his foul mood, he went through the motions, asking the newly sober guy about himself. The two of them soon opened up the Big Book and began reading at the place where they had left off in their step work. But Stanley was not feeling at all present, mentally. Instead, he was back at the tree, fuming about the barbed-wire, the city officials who had allowed such a thing to go unchecked, and the guy who had invented barbed wire in the first place.

As they wrapped up their hour-long session, to Stanley's total surprise, Sponsee #1 told him that he had never gotten so much out of one of their sessions. He felt that finally the Twelve Steps were starting to have an impact on his outlook, and he was so thankful he had found such a great sponsor. Stanley wasn't sure what to make of it, but he just assumed that the young buck was still a little wet-brained or something.

Then they attended an AA meeting together. Stanley was still annoyed, and the meeting made little impact on his mood. At the end of the meeting he met up with Sponsee #2. Stanley took the same approach, trying to be helpful but completely distracted. At the end of their time, Sponsee #2 said almost the same words to Stanley: "I've never gotten so much out of one of our meetings. The things you're saying make so much sense. You really know how to convey hope to me."

Needless to say, Stanley didn't know what to make of the whole experience at first. Upon reflection, however, he came to relay the following insight: "God's ability to be helpful through me is bigger than my bad mood's ability to torpedo His plans. God can use a sober alcoholic in a bad mood to help a person just as well as he can use a focused, inspired sober alcoholic for the same enterprise." Stanley's life was not his own. So much so in fact, that *he seemed unable to step outside of God's will for him.* This was a hugely helpful and humbling realization. It gave credit to the one who deserved it, not to the "earthen vessel" who happened to be carrying the goods (2 Cor 4:7).

The resolve of the 7th Step has more to do with living in God's grace *in spite of* the continual presence of defects of character than it does with living in their absence. Still full of bad moods, and yet owned by something bigger, a person's second narrative tells the real truth. This narrative operates over and above the sin of the individual, a spiritual covering of sorts. Gerhard Forde described this sentiment in a little piece he wrote toward the end of his life. He spoke from his own experience of the way in which 7th Step-type spirituality had altered his understanding of God's work in human life:

> "Am I making progress? If I am really honest, it seems to me that the question is odd, even a little ridiculous. As I get older and death draws nearer, it doesn't seem to get any easier. I get a little more impatient, a little more anxious about having perhaps missed what this life has to offer, a little slower, harder to move, a little more sedentary and set in my ways. It seems more and more unjust to me that now that I have spent a good part of

my life 'getting to the top,' and I seem just about to have made it, I am already slowing down, already on the way out. A skiing injury from when I was sixteen years old acts up if I overexert myself. I am too heavy, the doctors tell me, but it is so hard to lose weight! Am I making progress? Well, maybe it seems as though I sin less, but that may only be because I'm getting tired! It's just too hard to keep indulging the lusts of youth. Is that sanctification? I wouldn't think so! One should not, I expect, mistake encroaching senility for sanctification."[74]

Forde began that essay by summarizing this point in the following way: "sanctification is the art of getting used to justification." This is just a theological way of saying that growth in spiritual maturity involves an increasing sense of our sinfulness, coupled with a corresponding appreciation of God's graciousness to us. Any form of spirituality that neglects this humble understanding of how God transforms an individual has missed something very important.

Type 2: Yes, but...Yes!

"Which of you fathers, if your son asks for a fish, will give him a snake instead? Or if he asks for an egg, will give him a scorpion?
-Luke 11:11-12

Stand-up comedian Maria Bamford offers a somewhat cynical read on the over-spiritualization that she experiences on a regular basis in Los Angeles. She says:

---

[74] Gerhard O. Forde, "The Lutheran View of Sanctification", *The Preached God: Proclamation in Word and Sacrament*, Ed. Mark C. Mattes and Steven D. Paulson (Grand Rapids, MI: Eerdmans, 2007), 244, 230.

> "I live in LA, and a lot of my friends claim to be 'spiritual.' They have all these 'miracles' happening in their lives. The weird part about this, at least to my way of thinking, is that the Lord seems to be manifesting himself in all sorts of small parking and shopping-related miracles. [She parrots one of her friends:] 'So I pull up outside of The Gap and a parking space opens up right next to the mall entrance. So I say to myself, *Okay, if it's meant to be?* I go inside...and the sweater is 25% off! It's like, *Okay, I get it. I'm on the path...*'"

To Maria's way of thinking, her friends have unwittingly begun to baptize their own self-interest with the help of spiritual terminology.[75]

She is critiquing precisely the same inclinations that the Twelve Steps critique. Yet one wonders what her criteria for an answered prayer would be. If her friend were praying for a sick child to be healed, and the child experienced a surprising return to complete health in spite of dissenting medical speculation, would that count as a legitimate answer to prayer? One suspects that her comments betray a more deep-seeded doubt in the very possibility of a spiritual reality beyond our immediate perception.

Disappointments in our prayer life often bring us to see "unanswered" prayer in a completely different light. This is why people are encouraged to pray on a daily basis while paying as little attention as possible to whether or not the prayers are working. It

---

[75] Ludwig Feuerbach famously criticized this spiritualization of self-interest in religion, arguing in favor of atheism quite compellingly with the idea that any belief in God which aligns itself with our wishes is simple fantasy: "God is the love that satisfies our wishes, our emotional wants; he is himself the realised wish of the heart, the wish exalted to the certainty of fulfilment, of its reality... 'God is love': this, the supreme dictum of Christianity, only expresses the certainty that... the inmost wishes of the heart have objective validity and reality." (Ludwig Feuerbach, *The Essence of Christianity*, trans. George Eliot (Amherst, NY: Prometheus, 1989), 121.)

might sound like a rationalization, but it is profoundly good news that prayers almost never play out in ways that can be anticipated…except, that is, when they do. Sometimes God seems to say: "Sure. I was thinking the same thing." We turn our focus now to the Yes…but-yes side of a prayer life.

The Big Book encourages us to pray concretely about the things in our life that concern us. It also offers a single and far-reaching caveat which accounts nicely for what we'll call the Maria Bamford critique of spirituality cited above. As the Big Book cautions, "We may ask for ourselves…if others will be helped. We are careful never to pray for our own selfish ends. Many of us have wasted a lot of time doing that and it doesn't work. You can easily see why." The 7th Step encourages us to pray for ourselves so that we might better be able to serve God and our neighbors, not so that we can find nice sweaters at discounted prices.

It should come as no surprise that the founders of AA believed that, in many cases, God does indeed "remove our shortcomings." And they were not deluded to think so. We pray for God to remove our self-centeredness and find that our relationships with others and our ability to be of service increases exponentially. Or perhaps we pray about lust and find that we are not as preoccupied with lascivious thoughts throughout the day. Or maybe we have an illness and ask for God to heal us, only to find that, for no apparent reason, we soon feel substantially better. Implausible as they may be to some people, these things happen all the time.

While we do not base our belief in God upon such "God-instances," they are nonetheless an integral part of the spiritual awakening that occurs as a result of the Twelve Steps. Step 7 both opens the door to such positive developments and gives us the means to deepen spiritually when these developments do not seem to be occurring.

The Bible is full of examples of this principle. Most of Jesus' healings were straightforward: someone asked to be healed, and then they were healed. On the other hand, Jesus just as often worked in unexpected or even inscrutable ways. When two women asked him to heal their friend Lazarus, for instance, his lengthy delay allowed Lazarus to die, only after which Jesus resurrected him. We see the same two avenues in Acts: much of the narrative recounts the early church's persecution and difficulty, but at one point we read that "the churches were strengthened in the faith and grew daily in numbers." So examples of God straightforwardly bestowing his "favor" are not hard to find in the Bible. Yet as any AA will tell you, those times have not come to an end; they occur daily in the lives of sober alcoholics.

I might characterize this second way in which prayers are answered as the "Yes? ... *yes!*" variety. This is answered prayer in the most good-old-fashioned way conceivable: "I prayed God would remove my nervousness, and sure enough, the speech went swimmingly well and I felt a sense of peace the moment I got to the podium."

One of my favorite examples of the "yes?... *yes!*" answer to prayer came from a former sponsee named Elwood. Elwood was exceptionally bright, holding an advanced degree from an Ivy League school, but his drinking problem had caused both his personal life and his career to unravel. When I met him, he was unemployed and newly sober. While he had experienced floundering sobriety for a few months, Elwood was miserable and fraught with neurosis. We began the process of working through the Twelve Steps. He responded, as most miserable sober alcoholics do, like a fish to water.

One of Elwood's prominent character defects was his smoking. He chain-smoked ravenously, and his urge for nicotine dominated a substantial portion of his day. Furthermore, his smoking worried him. I encouraged him to smoke and not to worry about it, to focus his attention on working the Twelve Steps instead of on quitting. "We will get there," I told him.[76]

So Elwood worked his way through the steps vigorously, cranking out an incredibly thorough 4th Step. He started to become a bit happier, and his life slowly found a more solid footing. It wasn't long before a job interview turned up.

The morning of the interview Elwood woke up early, smoked ten cigarettes back-to-back, took a shower, put on a suit, Febreez'ed himself all over to destroy the slightest hint of a cigarette aroma and then went in to the interview. It went really well, and he was hired a few weeks later.

This precipitated a serious dilemma for him, because Elwood was convinced that being a smoker and being a successful banker were at odds with each other. He did not want anyone he worked with to even suspect him of smoking. Consequently, he developed an incredibly complex routine in the mornings that involved smoking half a pack of cigarettes and then cleaning himself up with a shower and a thorough deodorizing ritual. He would then work all day, white-knuckling his cravings away – with the help of secret stashes of Nicotine gum – only to return home immediately following the end of the work day, where he would smoke an entire pack of cigarettes before going to bed. He repeated this cycle day in and day out, and it was causing him serious misery.

It wasn't long after he got the job that we finished the 5th Step and compiled a list of character defects. At the top of his list was "smoking." While I tried to relinquish some of the guilt he felt about living a double life where nicotine was concerned, this did little good. I encouraged him to begin praying for God to remove his defects of character, including smoking, but not to try to quit in the meantime. Since his multiple attempts to quit smoking in

---

[76] With this comment to Elwood, I was anticipating Steps 6 and 7.

the past had failed, I encouraged him to smoke away, but to pray every day for God to remove "smoking." I suggested he do this for an entire year without trying to quit and Elwood agreed.

Every day, he started the day with a 7th Step prayer, asking God to remove his defects. Smoking, he said, was always at the forefront of his mind. Meanwhile, his insane ritual continued. I believe he even smoked while saying the prayer! Six months after we began going through the Twelve Steps, I moved away from New York and lost regular contact with him.

I had seen, even in that short time, how Elwood was being transformed by God's grace. He had begun to smile, to enjoy his life and his work. He even sponsored others and took them through the Twelve Steps.

A year and a half passed. One day I got an email from him, out of the blue. In it, he told me that after praying daily for eight months for God to remove his smoking, he visited a doctor who prescribed him a medication that alleviated some of the cravings. He had then been able, with the help of Nicotine gum *and* patches, along with the prescribed medication, to quit. He had not smoked a cigarette in almost a year. Not only that, but he was writing in part to ask if I would be willing to sponsor his upcoming run in the New York City marathon, which he was doing to raise money for a charity. He was overjoyed to relay all that had happened, and I was once again, bowled over by the awesome power of God and His ability to remove character defects outright.

In preparing to write this document, I contacted Elwood again via email. It had been four years since we had last been in touch. I informed him that I was in the middle of writing some reflections on the Twelve Steps, and that I always think about his story when I spoke on the 7th Step. I wondered if he was still a non-smoker.

He almost immediately responded, "I quit smoking six years ago and haven't looked back!" Sure enough, God had continued to answer that prayer in the best way we could have hoped for. When God decided it was time for the defect to be removed after eight months of prayer, Elwood quit. He couldn't even finish out the last four months of our agreement!

A 7th Step Epilogue

The word "remove" deserves a little more attention because it suggests the intriguing way in which God tends to work upon us. It implies that when a character defect is taken away, something else—something spiritual—is found beneath it or, rather, in its absence. The notion that we become more spiritual through deconstruction is not common, but it is helpful and true, to both life and Christianity.

The 7th Step suggests that God's work is primarily deconstructive and not constructive. He does not so much build us up as tear us down, in order to turn us into new people. We find this dynamic powerfully articulated in The 39 Articles of Religion, a series of 16th-Century theological propositions that formed the basis of the Protestant Anglican Church. Two of them are particularly relevant:

> "Good works spring out necessarily of a true and lively faith...but we have no power to do good works...without the grace of God *preventing* us, that we may have a good will, and working with us, when we have that good will" (Articles XII & X).

The word "preventing" implies that it is when God hinders us that we bear spiritual fruit in our actions.

Sometimes our confidence in our own efforts to change ourselves, as well as problems of pride and control that accompany such efforts, actually hinder spirituality. While we affirm the insight that "in serving God, there is perfect freedom", we also do well to wonder if His work in our lives occasionally limits our freedom to free us from the burden of selfhood, thereby allowing us to serve Him all the better.

Step 8

"Made a List of All Persons We Had Harmed, and Became Willing to Make Amends to Them All"

Step 8 has two familiar themes: the first involves making another list, this time of people to whom we need to make amends, and the second has to do with confronting one's unwillingness to accept what the list represents.

In the 8th Step, we simply make a list of the people we have harmed, if at all possible, without thinking about the emotional implications or logistical issues that might apply in any effort to make amends. We do not need to waste mental energy figuring out whether we can or should be able get in touch with these people – we just make the list. Step 8 and the actual making of amends should be treated as two completely separate things.

"Made a List..."

At this point, we've gathered a bit of experience with list-making, especially from the 4th Step. The person who listened to our 5th Step may well have encouraged us to make a substantial portion of an 8th Step list during that 5th Step session. When listening to a 5th Step, if I notice that the person mentioned in an inventory has been harmed by the behavior of the step-worker, I simply ask them to make a star or asterisk next to the name of the person. Then, at the end of the 5th Step, I encourage them to compile the names of all the people with stars next to their names into a fresh list. That list becomes the beginning of their 8th Step work.

Whom have we harmed with our self-centered behavior? Which people and institutions have been affected by our resentments? We write them down on a fresh piece of paper under the heading "Step 8." Again, some of the people on our lists are usually loved ones, spouses, siblings, and other family members.

Another category of people who should be featured on the list are people with whom we are "no longer speaking." What relationships have disintegrated due to differences of opinion or argument? Who did we used to be friends with? Did we contribute in some way to the collapse of that relationship? If the answer is yes, then we add them to the list. One helpful way to figure out who these people are involves using our imagination.

Imagine, for a moment, that you are sitting in a coffee shop. Picture all of the people you have ever known walking into the shop (including people who have died), one at a time. Ask yourself whether or not an interaction would be awkward. If you could keep the person from recognizing you, would you? Who would you cross the street to avoid? Is it because you have caused some kind of harm that amounted to a bridge-burning? Is there anyone that you hope you won't have to see again for the rest of your life?

It may be the case that restitution has already been made to a particular individual. Perhaps apologies have been made. Or maybe the victim of an action is "over it." We add those names to our list anyway in the spirit of thoroughness.

The Big Book points out that there is also a category of people or institutions who may not have made an appearance in a 4th Step but who nonetheless need to be featured on an 8th Step list. They are people whom we have harmed but do not resent, battles we have won. Often this category includes financial institutions or places to whom we have an outstanding debt. Bill is quick to remind us that "most alcoholics owe money" (78). Perhaps one of us stole something from a store and did not get caught. This incident may not have appeared in a 4th Step, but the action still caused harm to that institution. "We put them on paper, even though we had no resentment in connection with them" (68).

"...And Became Willing to Make Amends to Them All"

Here we come to the second part of Step 8, "becom[ing] willing to make amends to them all." This is the part that commonly outsmarts us. It shows us what we most need to see about ourselves, namely that we are un-willing to make amends.

The idea of reconnecting with the people whom we have wronged is uncomfortable – of course it is. But we need to be honest with ourselves about this fact instead of keeping it buried or trying to justify it. Here we see the general angle of spirituality again, that it goes against the grain of our instincts and thereby deflates our overgrown egos. Our reluctance reveals to us just how important the next step may be for us. The extent to which Step 8 makes us uncomfortable will be roughly equivalent to the relief that Step 9 brings. The discomfort points to a whole new world that God has for us. It points to a momentous amount of freedom from guilt, the kind of freedom that most people desperately need for mental health.

The Big Book wisely suggests that we enter into this place of reluctance through prayer: "If we haven't the will to do this, we ask until it comes" (76). The pathway to willingness begins with unwillingness. If we are reluctant to revisit past grievances, then we are unwilling to make amends. In the same way that we become "entirely ready" in Step 6, we become "willing" in Step 8. We therefore proceed by asking: which amends are we unwilling to make? Then we say a prayer about them, one which we think is just as useful for non-alcoholics. A simple 8th Step prayer goes as follows:

> "God, help me to see where it is that I am reluctant to let you help me. Please remove my unwillingness and my fears. Help me to become willing to make all the amends that You would have me make."

A Side Note: The Necessity of Amends (and Another A-Word)

"Forgive us our debts, as we forgive our debtors."
-Lord's Prayer, Matthew 6:12

A recognition of the power of guilt and remorse shapes the Twelve Steps. Indeed, the form of the Steps suggests that lasting sobriety (and spiritual health) occurs only to the extent that past regrets and trespasses have been addressed and, in some way, resolved. Once the most painful matters in a person's past have been processed, a sense of serenity will take their place.

Although the pervasive, irrepressible sense of guilt for past wrongs practically beats us over the head with the need for resolution, Step 8 acknowledges the persistent fact that *people are typically reluctant to revisit past grievances.* Instead, we prefer to sweep problems under the rug and pretend as if we have no outstanding sense of debt, thereby fostering a superficial sense of self-esteem. One of the main rules for radio broadcasting, for instance, is "never draw attention to your mistakes." But the rule has a much wider jurisdiction than the airwaves.

Where I live in South Carolina, a refined code of etiquette governs social interaction. In theory, the system can enable a person to avoid all awkwardness and unpleasantness with the utmost of ease. Upon meeting someone for the first time, for example, it is customary to say, "It's good to *see* you" rather than "It's good to *meet* you." "Meeting" implies that the other person was a complete stranger until the encounter happened. And to be a stranger is to be out of place, even to be in the wrong place. To "see" someone, on the other hand, implies kinship, mutual friends, and a shared social milieu.

In this sense, manners allow new facets of life to be incorporated gracefully into daily life, interpersonal distance to be downplayed, and discord and conflict to be circumvented. Consider manners, however, when it comes to the making of amends. How do they fit into a brutally awkward apology? Or what is their role in a coffeehouse meeting with a person whose life you nearly ruined years ago? Entering into places of personal sin and past suffering explodes the notion that mannered pleasantries can enable a person to actually deal substantively with any form of brokenness. In the same way, Step 8 and 9's confrontation with one's past crushes the illusion that we are able, through careful strategizing, to ignore or evade the ugly parts of life.

Another example of avoiding unpleasant interactions comes in the form of "boundary" talk. We may stake off a portion of our emotional landscape as being inaccessible to someone who has harmed us, walling ourselves off from sources of potential pain. We see this in romantic relationships that take breaks for a short, specified period of time – unsurprisingly, the problems that caused the break usually reemerge very quickly. Similarly, many children choose colleges or jobs far away from home to escape their overbearing parents, but this often just increases emotional distance without really solving the underlying problems.

Sometimes, people go so far as to cut ties with another person altogether. As a minister, I've discovered the sad truth that many funerals feature a startling absence of the deceased person's son, daughter, sister, or other immediate family. In some cases, this occurs with parents who have engaged in crime, marital infidelity, and other harmful (i.e. abusive) behaviors. In other cases, the adult children have simply made the decision to sever ties with their parents or siblings. While some situations seem broken beyond repair, and some indeed are, AA would still affirm that reconciliation is far healthier than a permanently closed door.

Again, relational difficulties cannot be sidestepped by either subtle or overt methods of avoidance. Pain and misfortune do not come from bad manners or wicked stepmothers, as much as we might sometimes wish they did. We cannot avoid the evil of our past by simply ignoring it. With sharp insight, Nobel Prize winning author Alexander Solzhenitsyn critiques this mentality of solving problems by avoiding them:

> "If only there were evil people somewhere insidiously committing evil deeds and it were necessary only to separate them from the rest of us and destroy them. But the line dividing good and evil cuts through the heart of

every human being. And who is willing to destroy a piece of his own heart?"[77]

The same could apply to our desire to suppress memories of the harm we've committed in the past. Even if we do try to pretend our mistakes away, the more egregious ones have a way of forcing themselves to the surface of our conscience. In fact, past hurts are substantial precisely to the extent that they cannot be swept under the rug. The alcoholic whose life has imploded often tries to turn a blind eye and create a pretend-world where things 'are not really *that* bad.' The wreckage a newly sober alcoholic faces, however, eventually demands confrontation: past offenses and sufferings, like a trail of breadcrumbs to a bird, eventually leads him into the rooms of AA. Once there, the alcoholic concretely encounters the universal need for reconciliation with his past. For this reason, it is sometimes said in AA that, "it's not drinking that brings a person to AA; it's trouble."

In this sense, AA's head-on approach for dealing with shameful and embarrassing events lacks the superficiality of more conventional approaches, which tend to either minimize the wrong or offer some flimsy version of self-absolution. Not surprisingly, it is also this driving force of extreme honesty that undergirds the recognition of both our guilt and our need in Christianity.

The Gospel message exposes the notion that we can move gracefully through all of life as a myth, one in which we pretend to play the role of the righteous, conquering hero. No one can or does live without regret, and the universality of our guilt confirms this insight. Rather than opting for an illusory feeling of blamelessness, *Christianity assumes our guilt...and forgives it.*

---

[77] Alexander Solzhenitsyn, *The Gulag Archipelago* (William Collins, Sons: Glasgow, 1974), 168.

By implication, it's not hard to understand why the Gospel message places so much emphasis upon the cross: it is the place where debts are paid and sins forgotten, where God reconciles Himself to sinful men and women. Suffering and guilt are not avoided; rather, the cross confronts them, bears them, and resolves them. Jesus didn't pretend that everything was all right with people. Instead, he identified with human sin so much that the New Testament writer says he was "made to be sin" itself for our sake (2 Cor 5:21). Were it not for guilt, Jesus could have died painlessly in old age. True forgiveness and reconciliation requires an honest confrontation of the problem, both in Christianity and in daily, Step 8 life. This will sound exceedingly harsh to those who are convinced they can live an unblemished existence. It is unromantic in the extreme. But it brings us to two crucial points about amends-making.

First, AA and Christianity agree on the universal need for reconciliation with one's past. As William Faulkner said, "the past is never dead. It's not even past."[78] Living a truly peaceful life in the present requires resolution. Christianity does this with the death and resurrection of Christ; AA does it with amends-making.

Christian theology understands the cross to have made true, real, and living amends – one which actually removes guilt and makes us innocent before God. AA amends, on the other hand, are merely a horizontal shadow of this vertical reality. Despite their often conciliatory effects, Step 9 amends do not attempt to undo the past wrong so much as therapeutically to ameliorate its impact on the victim. To do this requires direct, often face-to-face acknowledgment with the person harmed.

Indeed, amends-making consists of surrender before the other person, a surrender that comes from a confrontation with

---

[78] William Faulkner, *Requiem for a Nun* (New York, NY: Random House, 1950), I.3.

one's own guilt. It is a place of death, in other words. Both AA and Christianity, in this sense, locate our best hope for peace in the death of our delusions of blamelessness, that is, in our unveiling before the person or standard we have violated. The peace and fulfillment that amends-makers often receive from Steps 8 and 9 flow out of the painful, experiential, concrete confession of one's sin in an interpersonal context.

The need to have our guilt forgiven defines the movement of the steps accordingly.[79] For some of us, the importance of amends-making points to a larger, more existential need for forgiveness and reconciliation.

It may not be a fashionable sentiment, but as our lives and relationships and the Twelve Steps and the Bible attest, the balance sheet needs setting straight. The dream of accomplishing this through our performance is just that: a dream. Minimizations, evasions, and justifications will not do the trick either. In God's grace, however, there is a wider net. It is one that can handle anything that swims its way. In Christianity, forgiveness is the final word.[80] It transforms a heart and, were it more present in the world, it might alter the plight of humanity. Steps 8 and 9 assume as much.

---

[79] The theological word for this is 'atonement.' One of the chief ways of understanding this in Christian theology is through the image of the law court. In this account, the mechanism of Christian salvation is above all one of God, in a sort of divine 'courtroom', passing judgment over humanity for its sins. Out of love, Christ, who is sinless, steps in as a substitute to be judged in place of the sinner. This substitution is understood primarily in terms of the satisfaction of God's justice through a transfer of merit. The result is that a person's sin is forgiven, God's favor is restored, and the way to eternal life is opened. Where amends are concerned in AA, the goal is a kind of horizontal reconciliation, spurred on by the (vertical) inclination of God's greater good will. The Christian faith undeniably turns the volume up on such a picture of things, seeing the cross of Christ to be the ultimate locus for all reconciliation between that which is broken and a God who is holy.

[80] As the Reverend John D. ("Jady") Koch puts it, "The judgment of God is forgiveness."

Step 9

"Made Direct Amends to Such People Wherever Possible Except when to Do So Would Injure Them or Others."

Step 9 is the amends-making step. It scares the daylights out of people. It involves making restitution for past harms. But the Twelve Step version of an apology is a very stylized thing, much more than a simple 'sorry' and much more effective too. Step 9 is where we learn how to mend broken relationships.

The Purpose of Amends

"Our real purpose is to fit ourselves to be of maximum service to God and the people about us."
-Big Book (77)

A newly healed bone is strongest at the point where it was broken, or so the conventional wisdom goes. Step 9 bears this out. Indeed, broken relationships and past harms provide us with a fantastic opportunity to grow in the experience of God's grace. The injured places in our lives are where healing and new life are most readily attainable.

We have begun to see how this is true in our own lives, but seeing how it is true in the lives of others — and how we can play a role in bringing it about — is one of the greatest blessings found in the Twelve Steps. You will not want to miss Step 9. As the Big Book tells us, "If we are painstaking about this phase of our development, we will be amazed before we are halfway through" (83).

As we find new footing with God through the Twelve Steps, it is remarkable how we become able to help our neighbors do the same. To the extent that we have harmed other people, we have stifled and frustrated their ability to have peace in that area of their lives. Imagine a person's life as it moves along a single dotted line from one point to the next. At the moment where my line intersects with that of another person, my negative impact halts the ease with which he is able to continue along an unimpeded path. Like a river that hits a rock, his trajectory is forcibly rerouted. The rock in question is what we call harm. And while people clearly learn to compensate for the harm we have caused them, compensation is not the same thing as healing.

Step 9 is where we enable those we have hurt to progress past the harm we have caused. The amend functions like the untangling of a knot in a piece of thread. With Step 9, the bad begins to heal, but any good that may have developed in wake of the harm remains as well. It's a classic win-win.

Maybe it's not surprising to discover that our lives are being straightened out for the sake of others, but Step 9 drives this reality home. The Big Book describes the process as being, "fitted to be of maximum service to God and the people about us" (77). In this sense, amends are not primarily designed to give us relief from guilt; they exist instead for the sake of the people to whom we are making them. After all, love will always emphasize the wellbeing of others over and against our own. Yet if we make amends correctly, we will usually experience an incredible new freedom and resolution with our past. Plus, there is the joy of knowing that we have tried our best to give the other person an opportunity to sort through the wreckage we caused. Making amends actually helps to shore up our future against many of the pitfalls that have dragged us down in the past.

The Making of Amends Does Not Begin with the Making of Amends

If we have made it this far in the program, chances are that we've started making amends without even being aware of the technicalities of Step 9. An increased desire to acknowledge shortcomings and apologize quickly is part of the fruit that comes from working the Steps.

But it is also the case that external factors play a role in creating this readiness to make amends. Perhaps you hear from an old acquaintance out of the blue, or bump into someone you haven't seen in years. Many a recovering alcoholic has reported that the Steps almost seem to be happening *to* them, of their own accord, and nowhere is this more apparent than with Step 9. I knew one AA who found himself seated on a plane next to one of the people on his 8th Step list, just a week after finishing his 5th Step. *When it's time for this sort of healing to occur, God often makes it obvious*, both by preparing us and the recipients for amends-making. Which is not to say that we should ever recklessly make amends without serious reflection and consultation with a sponsor. Fresh enthusiasm is not the same thing as wisdom. Step 9 has as much new material to teach us as any of the other steps.

Amends-making ideally begins with a talk with your sponsor or spiritual mentor. As a general principle, *we avoid making any amends that we have not run by an understanding person first.* Our sponsor will be able to help us figure out how to make amends to the people on our list.[81] Personal experience, filtered through the 4th step moral inventory, has likely taught us to be skeptical about our knee-jerk inclinations. How often we have heard about the newly sober alcoholic, eager to connect with an ex-girlfriend, who has used Step 9 as an excuse for doing so. Few and far between are the sponsors who would encourage us to start our amends-making by calling up an ex!

The other desire that we hope to counteract is the urge to make amends for selfish reasons and at the expense of another's well-being. Airing past grievances can be a huge relief, but it is not always helpful. To the extent that doing so is unhelpful, it is probably not a good idea. For instance, a wise sponsor would probably discourage someone from telling tell his 85-year-old grandmother that he – the apple of her eye – has just gotten sober after a long battle with drug addiction and incarceration. This is the "except when to do so would injure them or others" part of Step 9. While he may wish to tell the whole world about the newfound freedom he is enjoying, the news may not be received as warmly by those who have been protected from his ruckus

---

[81] For those doing application with this step: if you don't have a sponsor or person to run this list by, it's a good idea to go through the next section where we describe much of the material that a sponsor or the Big Book would offer. Using common sense, try to figure out which type of amend each person on your list should receive, and proceed accordingly. But please be on the lookout for a person, perhaps a buddy from a Bible study, who you can bring into your life in this way. They might be just as eager to 'try on' the Twelve Steps themselves if presented with the opportunity.

behavior. To them, the revelation about his past may prove jarring, *especially* when sobriety is a particularly recent development. Someone would do much better revealing this material after many years of sobriety.

The guiding sensation behind these kinds of novice actions is not unlike the urge that drives gossip and the telling of secrets. There may be a natural desire to do so, but it is almost always a bad idea. The Big Book considers this matter carefully. Where is truth-telling at odds with love? Considers the example of adultery:

> "A man so involved often feels very remorseful at times, especially if he is married to a loyal and courageous girl who has literally gone through hell for him. Whatever the situation, we usually have to do something about it. If we are sure our wife does not know, should we tell her? Not always, we think. If she knows in a general way that we have been wild, should we tell her in detail? Undoubtedly we should admit our fault. She may insist on knowing all the particulars. She will want to know who the woman is and where she is. We feel we ought to say to her that we have no right to involve another person. We are sorry for what have done and, God willing, it shall not be repeated. More than that we cannot do; we have no right to go further. Though there may be justifiable exceptions, and though we wish to lay down no rule or any sort, we have often found this the best course to take...Good generalship may decide that the problem should be attacked on the flank rather than risk a face-to-face combat" (80-82).

Notice that with amends-making, the well-being of others is always the primary concern. There is occasionally a tension between trying to make amends in order to allay our own guilt and making them for the good of another; when this tension arises, we may err in the direction of the former, selfish way. Again, the stickiness and complexity of our past (and our own feelings about it) is simply another reason why the wise counsel of another is almost always beneficial.

Truth be told, the pitfalls associated with amends-making are almost impossible to avoid completely without God's help. We have learned that such help often comes through the mouth of other people. If we waited until our motivations were perfect, we would wait forever. Rather than let these pitfalls deter us, therefore, perhaps they can inspire us to test the substance of having God at the center of our lives – such an attitude rarely disappoints. "Into your hands I commit my spirit" makes for a good motto during the amends-making process (Psalm 31:5, quoted by Christ on the cross in Luke 23:46).

How to Make Amends: Four Kinds of Amends

There are four types of amends described in Step 9 of the *12 & 12*. They are: 1) the face-to-face amend, 2) the wait-and-see-but-be-willing amend, 3) the letter/email amend, and 4) the living amend. At the start of Step 9, preferably with the help of a sponsor, each name on your 8th Step list should be grouped into one of these four categories. Let's look at each of them.

1) Face-to-Face

The face-to-face amend is the bread-and-butter of the 9th Step. It's the classic. Chances are that you've actually heard stories of members of AA making amends to someone you know. You may even have been the recipient of one yourself.

After we've figured out which of our amends fit into this category, we're encouraged to dive right in and make them as quickly as possible. If people are not sure which one to start with, I sometimes repeat the advice that one sponsor gave to me: "Start with the scariest one first." Having fun yet?

Once we've settled on a name, the first thing that needs to be done (with every type of amend) is prayer. Perhaps something along the lines of, *"God, please help me to make amends to N. in a way that is beneficial to him and to you. Amen."*

Following the prayer, we try contacting the person either by email or phone. We do not make the amend over the phone; we simply set up the opportunity to connect with them. Coffee shops typically make fantastic settings. The invitation to meet up may receive an abrupt "no way, (Jerk!)", or no response at all. If we do not hear back from the person after a week has gone by, we might ask our sponsor if we should try getting in touch one more time. If we are not encouraged to do so, we consider our work with that one name on the list to be "done" for the time being. We never know; we may hear from that person two months or even two years later, at which point we will know it's time to make the amend. We do not say to ourselves, "Oh well, she didn't reply to my email within a week of my sending it, so I now have nothing to say to her. You snooze, you lose!" Step 9 only shows us how to begin the process of healing our broken relationships – it does not end the process.

But let's say the person is willing to meet. To understand how recovering alcoholics are encouraged to go about amends-making, imagine for a moment that you're the one making an amend. Your goal is to put the person at ease, which means you want to be especially sensitive to the fact that he may not really want to meet with you even though he has consented to do so. Tread lightly, in other words, and do not assume that you are now about to meet a new best friend. That is unlikely.

Let's say you meet her at a coffee shop. While the situation may vary slightly from case to case, in general most sponsors would have you follow something close to these guidelines:

First, you say a prayer before the time you are to meet with them. Next, you get to the meeting place early so as not to inconvenience the person in any way. You might offer to buy her coffee if she wants some. Make light small talk and reassure them with a smile and calm demeanor. You are not there to pounce, which would likely be the exact way you got yourself into needing to make amends in the first place.

After a few short minutes, the person will make it clear (using body language or perhaps words) that she is ready to hear why you have called her to the rendezvous. You would then say something like the following:

> "Thank you for meeting with me. I've been trying to make some changes in my life, and part of those changes has involved a fair amount of reflection. I'm aware that I have not treated some of the people in my life well, and I think you are one of them. Looking back, I see that there were times in our past when I acted selfishly. It was not fair to you, and I regret it. I've asked you to meet me here today so that I could tell you I'm sorry for the way I acted and the things I did. Is there anything I can do to make it up to you?"

Notice that the amends-maker does not initially need to highlight any particular incident. After we have said our piece, we should shut our mouths and allow the other person to process what we have said. We should listen to whatever he has to say. We encourage amends-makers not to be afraid of silence. We are not looking for any particular response, other than the one which comes naturally to the recipient. God will guide the other person.

The recipient may or may or may not wish to revisit the past with us. Obviously the 9th Step creates a somewhat awkward interaction. The recipient may wish to move on quickly, demurring with a line like, "Don't worry about it. I forgive you. I'm glad you're doing well…" If this is the response, it's a fine one. After all, we only want the response that God gives him.

Another common response is, "What exactly are you talking about?" If this is the case, we might speak in brief, general terms about the particular circumstance involved (e.g., remember when we were in Spain? Or remember when we went on that double date…?). A short answer should be enough to trigger a more in-depth response, which is the very thing you are looking for.

The recipient may reply, "Well, I'm glad you're finally aware of how your behavior affected me. It was really upsetting!…" We allow him to vent, taking whatever poison he wishes to throw at us. In no case are we to discuss the recipient's behavior. Criticism of him has no place in Step 9. We are there to sweep off our side of the street, not his. As the book reminds us, "His faults are not discussed" (78).

People should feel free to plan what they want to say in advance. You could use the script above if you like, or you could create your own as long as the basic elements are covered: we are there to apologize for the harm we caused, acknowledging that we know we behaved badly and that we realize it was selfish. We regret it. And then we ask if there is anything we can do to mend the tear. "Is there anything I can do to make it up to you?" Even if there's nothing we can do, the other person will hopefully recognize that we know sincerely we have wronged them. If someone does request we make it up to them, we do so as best we can and within reason. These are the building blocks of an effective 9th Step amend.

2) The Letter

Making amends by writing a letter is a common and helpful practice when a face-to-face meeting is not possible. Perhaps a person on the list lives far away and cannot make a trip just to settle with you.[82] In that case, a brief letter or email may be appropriate, in which we acknowledge our wrong-doing and let the person know that we would like to make it up if there is any way to do so, covering the same essential bases mentioned in the face-to-face section above, but in written form. It need not be very long. If we have run the situation by our sponsor and have been advised to proceed with the writing of a 9th Step letter, we might read it to the sponsor before we send it.

One classic situation that merits an amend letter is the occasion of a death. Perhaps we treated a loved one horribly at a much earlier point in life, and then the loved one died. Obviously we cannot make amends face-to-face. But perhaps we can visit the grave and read aloud what we would say in a face-to-face interaction. This can be very powerful.

Letters can also be helpful in cases where a person doesn't want to talk—but only if a sponsor advises us to do so. If a person does not wish to be in touch at all, it's probably wise not to press the issue. We might write an unsent letter and read it to a sponsor, to a counselor or minister, or quietly in a church to God during a mid-week lunch break.[83] Amends-makers sometimes pretend that the person is there and that they are able to talk, even though they

---

[82] Members of AA will often take a "9th Step Trip", revisiting places they used to live with the express purpose of making a series of amends. It's a great endeavor, but obviously it's good to set up as much of it as possible in advance.

[83] Consider a historic parallel: when David was unable to make amends to a person he had ordered killed, he wrote Psalm 51 to God instead: "I know my transgressions, and my sin is always before me. Against you, you only, have I sinned"

are not. The experience may sound a bit hokey, but it can be very helpful and cathartic. Additionally, someone's reluctance to be in contact with us may be God's way of telling us to proceed with a *living amend.*

Types 3 & 4: The "Living Amend" and the Wait-and-See-but-Willing Amend

If an amends-maker and his sponsor, mentor, or spiritual advisor have decided that some of the amends on the list should be postponed for whatever reason, then for the time being it becomes a "living amend." Perhaps you cannot approach an ex-girlfriend without arousing a certain amount of jealousy from either her spouse or his. In the case where making a face-to-face amend would cause more harm than good, the living amend becomes the best way to move forward.

Living amends involve creative ways of making restitution without doing additional harm. In one case, I remember consulting with a newly sober individual who had at times used drugs while working as a teacher. She felt terrible about the fact that she had acted in such a way, but we concluded that she would not be able to help her former students or their parents by bringing to light what she had done years after the fact. So the living amend became the advised approach. Keeping in stride with the 9th Step, she found an opportunity to volunteer as a tutor at a local school. This course of action provided her with peace of mind, a fantastically productive opportunity, and a reminder of how she had, in fact, been changed by God's grace.

Despite the focus on action and personal initiative, all four kinds of amends are different from self-reliance because they are somewhat uncomfortable on the front end. In a sense, we take the wrong we have inflicted upon another person and bear it ourselves, as much as possible. It is by willingly undergoing the awkward, mostly passive, embarrassing process of amends-making that we can bear some of the pain from past actions ourselves and, in so doing, help the other person to move on.

In most cases, the living amend is the opportunity to do the converse of what we did to cause the harm. It's the new good – in exchange for the old bad, something the *Book of Common Prayer* calls "newness of life." For example, it may be the opportunity to treat people the opposite of the way we used to treat them, to no longer be a cheat, or a thief, or a womanizer.

While there are a million different reasons why a living amend might be called for, fear is not one of them. Fear tends to underscore the need we have to make the amend, and it is rarely a good reason to avoid a direct amend in favor of the living one. Ask God to remove your fear and discuss the situation with your sponsor.

Money

The *12 & 12* adds "money" to the inventory list in Step 4, but we think it's a topic better suited for Step 9. This is because money is an unavoidable aspect of amends-making. For example, all debt is an outstanding amend that needs to be made. Most alcoholics owe money, and many of us have, at times in our lives, stolen in some fashion. How should monetary amends be made? For starters, probably not by the family man who is sole provider for a wife and kids putting himself forward for imprisonment over prior financial deceitfulness. Someone who has stolen, however, might send some anonymous cash to the department store from which she shoplifted. Many people do this exact kind of thing multiple times during Step 9. Someone else might tip hugely for a year at a certain restaurant where he used to work, one where he stole food, drinks, or money. I remember one sponsee who arranged a payment plan with his mother after he sobered up. Each month he gave her $200 until an agreed-upon amount had been reimbursed in its entirety. The advice of a third party in these matters is crucial – and willingness is indispensable.

The Making of Amends Does Not End With the Making of Amends

The 9th Step gives us an opportunity to lean upon our newfound trust in God. In my experience it is where the most enjoyable fruits of the spiritual life are found. Typically, the results of amends-making are edifying and wonderfully unpredictable. As the book says, "in nine cases out of ten the unexpected happens" (78).

By making an effort to repair the damage of our past conduct, we open the door to new events. People will rarely require us to do anything specific in response to an amend, unless perhaps monetary debt is involved. But it is important to realize that while the making of an amend begins with the 9th Step, it does not end there. Sometimes, a person to whom we have made an amend will contact us a week or so after the initial approach and say something like, "I know I said to forget about it, but since we met, there's one thing that I've been wanting to say about what happened all those years ago…" Our job in this situation is to listen and apologize in whatever way we can in good conscience. This may happen more than once.

In other instances, the amend may involve taking on a new approach with a family member. We may have to begin the long, slow process of trying to act differently each year at Christmas. We may have to start sending birthday cards or making regular phone calls home, even though the calls themselves sometimes feel like torture. Nonetheless, we take these hits as best we can, gladly turning the other cheek: "…with a person we dislike, we take the bit in our teeth. It is harder to go to an enemy than to a friend, but we find it much more beneficial to us" (77).

Three Examples of the 9th Step

"In nine cases out of ten the unexpected happens. Sometimes the man we are calling upon admits his fault, so that feuds of years' standing melt away in an hour. Rarely do we fail to make satisfactory progress. Our former enemies sometimes praise what we are doing and wish us well. Occasionally, they will offer assistance. It should not matter, however, if someone does throw us out of his office. We have made our demonstration, done our part."
-Big Book (78)

The good news of the 9th Step is that despite the awkwardness and emotional intensity of the amends-making process, healing is almost always the end result. Fresh starts occur. Second, third, and fiftieth chances are given. Grace is extended and received liberally in the world of Step 9. In more cases than not, huge strides toward newfound peace are taken.

But occasionally, this doesn't happen. The book mentions that we may be thrown out of an office as part of Step 9. I experienced my own version of this when I approached the manager of a radio station I had worked for a few years earlier. I walked into the station with a bag full of over 50 compact discs that I had stolen from the station's archives. I asked to speak with the manager, who ushered me into his office. I said my bit: I had stolen these CDs when I worked for the station; I was sorry and wished to return them and find out if there was anything else I could do to make it up.

His response caught me off-guard: "Who else stole music from us? I know there were others!" I told him that I did not know about anyone else and was not there to incriminate others, but that I had indeed stolen a lot of CDs while I worked there. He replied that if I could not name anyone else, he would be forced to ban me from the station "for the rest of [my] life." He pointed to the door. I accepted this punishment and have never returned to their offices (though I have listened to their station from my car on occasion, which I have decided is okay).

Fortunately, that's not what usually happens. The writers of the Big Book wished to share one of their favorite examples of the 9th Step, concerning a businessman who had acted unethically:

> "While drinking, he accepted a sum of money from a bitterly-hated business rival, giving him no receipt for it. He subsequently denied having received the money and used the incident as a basis for discrediting the man. He thus used his own wrongdoing as a means of destroying the reputation of another. In fact, his rival was ruined.
>
> He felt that he had done a wrong he could not possibly make right. If he opened that old affair, he was afraid it would destroy the reputation of his partner, disgrace his family and take away his means of livelihood. What right had he to involve those dependent upon him? How could he possibly make a public statement exonerating his rival?
>
> After consulting with his wife and partner he came to the conclusion that it was better to take those risks...He saw that he had to place the outcome in God's hands or he would soon start drinking again, and all would be lost anyhow. He attended church for the first time in many years. After the sermon, he quietly got up and made an explanation. His action met widespread

approval, and today he is one of the most trusted citizens of his town." (80)

A final illustration of amends-making comes from NBC's television show *Parenthood*. In that series, viewers have been introduced to a single mother, Sarah, and her two teenage children. Her ex-husband, Seth, abandoned the family when the children were very young, leaving her to raise them by herself. We are told simply that he was a musician with a terrible substance-abuse problem. On a few occasions during the sweep of the narrative, he re-emerges and wants to see his kids, apologizing for the harm he has caused them, only to then abandon them when he takes off on another bender.

In the third season of the show, Seth checks himself into a rehabilitative hospital, finally serious about sobering up and getting his life together. But his teenage kids are skeptical, and their guard is up; they have been hurt and disappointed too many times before. Sarah's parents are understandably very uncomfortable about Seth causing more trauma to their daughter and grandchildren. Plus, Sarah has a nice new boyfriend, who is somewhat turned off by the whole situation, and everyone is worried that Seth will chase him away.

When "Dad" finally makes it out of rehab, his daughter allows him to crash on her couch for a few nights, making it clear to him that the best way he can make amends to her and her brother and mother is to stay sober for a while. Seth sees that his presence is jeopardizing Sarah's budding relationship and bringing unwanted tension into his former in-laws' home, and knows he has to leave town.

Before he does, he finds a birthday card that he wrote to his daughter on her eighth birthday in a drawer in her kitchen, the only birthday card that he ever gave her.

The next day his daughter returns home from work to find that her dad has indeed left. You can see the relief on her face. She then notices something on her kitchen table: two manila envelopes, one bearing her name and the other her brother's. She opens the envelope to find nineteen birthday cards, one for every year except her eighth birthday. Inside each one is handwritten note from her father. She sits at the table reading through all of the cards from her father that she never got, and as she reads them she cries. The tears stream down her face, and the healing is palpable. As I watched it, I cried right along with her. It is a perfect portrait of amends-making, one which incorporates all four of the Step 9 categories we have been discussing.

The Twelve Steps bring with them a series of "promises." The most famous set of promises come at the end of the Big Book's section on Step 9. It is right that we too close this section with them:

> "If we are painstaking about this phase of our development, we will be amazed before we are half way through. We are going to know a new freedom and a new happiness. We will not regret the past nor wish to shut the door on it. We will comprehend the word serenity and we will know peace. No matter how far down the scale we have gone, we will see how our experience can benefit others. That feeling of uselessness and self-pity will disappear. We will lose interest in selfish things and gain interest in our fellows. Self-seeking will slip away. Our whole attitude and outlook upon life will change. Fear of people and of economic insecurity will leave us. We will intuitively know how to handle situations which used to baffle us. *We will suddenly realize that God is doing for us what we could not do for ourselves."* (83-84)

III: GROWING INTO GRACE

Step 10

"Continued to Take Personal Inventory and when We Were Wrong Promptly Admitted It."

"The sacrifice of the Ego elements must be total, or they will soon regain their ascendancy."
-Dr. Tiebout, *"Ego Factors of Surrender in Alcoholism"*

The spiritual life that we discover in the Twelve Steps has little to do with avoiding mistakes. It is much more concerned with how we deal with our mistakes once we make them or, you might say, with our mistake-making selves. As Chuck T. bluntly put it: "You'll never be so perfect that you don't have a crack in your a**!" In the preceding Steps we've learned a new set of skills—how to take a moral inventory, how to pray for God to remove our defects, how to make amends--and Step 10 weaves much of what we've learned together into a single reiteration.

The opening word of Step 10, "continued", is somewhat off-putting. It brings to mind all of the failed New Year's resolutions that have ever been attempted. Most of the time, it seems the character defects that have plagued our lives are the only things we have managed to keep up with any consistency.

Yet Step 10 introduces us to the ongoing reality of the spiritual life. Can we maintain? Of course, in a simple sense, the answer is no. We are bound to lapse on some front at some point. So we are warned in the same step about the times "when we were wrong", implying that even in sobriety, we will be "wrong." In AA, people often say, "With Step 10, it's *when* and not *if*." A return to the state of being in the wrong is imminent.

The Ego That Wouldn't Die

We never grow out of our need for Step 10. It never becomes extraneous or irrelevant. This is because the ego, which functions like a wedge between our selves and our appreciation of God, constantly seeks to rebuild itself. The great psychiatrist and friend of Bill Wilson, Dr. Harry Tiebout, wrote extensively about the ego's irrepressibility. In his prescient essay *The Ego Factors of Surrender in Alcoholism*, he writes:

> "Therapy is centered on the ways and means, first, of bringing the Ego to earth, and second, keeping it there. The discussion of this methodology would be out of place here, but it is relevant to emphasize one point, namely the astonishing capacity of the Ego to pass out of the picture and then reenter it, blithe and intact."

Next, and quite wonderfully, he draws attention to the Christian roots behind AA's concern for deflating the ego:

"It is the Ego which is the arch-enemy of sobriety, and it is the Ego which must be disposed of if the individual is to attain a new way of life…Life without Ego is no new conception. Two thousand years ago, Christ preached the necessity of losing one's life in order to find it again. He did not say Ego, but that was what he had in mind…As one sees this struggle in process, the need for the helping hand of a Deity becomes clearer. Mere man alone all too often seems powerless to stay the force of his Ego. He needs assistance and needs it urgently."[84]

Put It All Together and What Do You Get?

Step 10 calls us to keep doing the things we have already been doing. When a resentment arises, for example, we pray for it to be removed and focus on how we can be helpful to the person we resent. If the resentment does not budge, we write an inventory, looking at our part and then sharing it with a sponsor or another wise person. This allows us to keep track of how particular defects from our 6th Step list have re-emerged, and in that eventuality, we add the removal of these defects to our daily list of prayer requests. If we have acted out against the person with whom we are angry, we can also ask our sponsor whether or not amends should be made. Steps 4 – 9 are tools that we can carry with us into the future.

The *12 & 12* suggests a few different ways to work Step 10. Again, most importantly, we continue to take inventory, observing new resentments, fears, or sex problems when they crop up in our

---

[84] Harry M. Tiebout, "The Ego Factors of Surrender in Alcoholism", *Quarterly Journal on Studies of Alcohol*, December (1954).

lives. Hopefully, this constant reiteration of Steps 4 – 9 will become habitual. As the Big Book encouragingly describes, "What used to be the hunch or the occasional inspiration gradually becomes a working part of the mind" (87). We start to sense God's involvement in our lives because of the way He enables us to see our limitations. In other words, the Steps have given us a new perspective and a new understanding of ourselves.

Similarly, we may find that we value forgiveness more than we once did, confident that it is the only way to live at peace with our enemies—even if we are not able to do so on our own power. Consequently, we begin to seek God's help more of the time. It's hard to imagine that such an inclination could ever overreach itself. We are describing the actual "easier softer way" of doing life (58).

One major Step 10 tradition is the nightly inventory, taken at the end of the day:

> "When we retire at night, we constructively review our day. Were we resentful, selfish, dishonest or afraid? Do we owe an apology? Have we kept something to ourselves which should be discussed with another person at once? Were we kind and loving toward all? What could we have done better? (86)"

Many people choose to begin their evening inventory on their knees at the foot of their bed, with the prayer, "God, please show me what it is about my day that you would have me see." Then we replay the day in our minds. What did we do? Who did we interact with? Were there any important phone calls or emails? As we remember each particular interaction, we might briefly say a prayer for these people, "Dear Lord, please be with N. and help *him* with

Y. And if there's anything I can do in the future to be of service to *him*, please help me to become aware of it."[85]

Others may prefer to do their evening inventory in written form. Over time, such a journal often inadvertently turns into a record of answered prayers, which can be very meaningful to flip through. We realize how God has helped in each of the situations that used to concern us: "Wow! I remember when I was totally consumed about _____. It's been months since I have even thought about it!"

As we make our nightly review, we may find that one or two events from the day stand out uncomfortably. It may be that a set of circumstances remain unresolved. Pray about those circumstances. It might also be the case that we did something we regret, that we wish we could undo, or that we could have done better. Here we ask for God's help in the future with similar situations or with a particular person. We might also consider whether or not there is anything further we need to do as a result of the prickly instance. Do we owe an amend, or do we need to run the situation by another person?

Another form of inventory that the *12 & 12* describes is known as the "annual or semi-annual housecleaning" (89). This is where we take a bit of a retreat to review and inventory a larger chunk of time. This annual or semi-annual inventory is also useful for slow-building resentments that, like rolling snowballs, gradually accumulate in our lives. Again, for AA step work is continual.

Because this inventory process is so critical, we cannot do it alone. A big part of Step 10 has to do with keeping at least one other person abreast of our progress and the things in our lives

---

[85] Praying for people is a wonderful thing we can do for the people in our lives. It is a very practical thing, and usually requires few words. Just pray about the things you see that are going on in a particular person's life, expressing your concern and care, while putting their future in God's hands. You might visualize the person you wish to pray for standing in the palm of a huge hand.

that are most pressing, a la Step 5. Have we found some new friends who are going through the same type of reorientation? If not, they can almost always be found at any Twelve Step group or church Bible Study. If we have not made some new friends since beginning working the Twelve Steps, something is amiss. "Going it alone in spiritual matters is dangerous" (*12 & 12*, 60). Personally, I live by the following maxim and associate it with my experience of working the Twelve Steps: "Make sure that at least one person, but not the whole world, is abreast of everything that is going on in my life. No more secrets about myself."

"The Steps Work So Well That I Don't Do Them All the Time."

"Being still inexperienced and having just made conscious contact with God, it is not probable that we are going to be inspired at all times... We alcoholics are undisciplined. So we let God discipline us in the simple way we have just outlined."
-*Big Book (87-88)*

Let's not be fooled—we *will* botch the job of recovery. We will say the wrong thing, we will offend people unintentionally. We will make poor decisions, and we will make them for selfish reasons. Our egos will re-emerge. We will have days when we feel not at all spiritual. This is a normal part of being a human. To quote one old-timer: "Some days all I am is just sober." That is, some days he feels the absence of alcohol more than the presence of any kind of serenity. These are the realities of sin in a fallen world. Step 10 starts from that place. It understands, and it offers a way through the missteps and laziness.

Step 10 assumes that the Twelve Steps *will* work as well as they *have* worked. We do not need to acquire more skills; we only need to keep using the ones we have already learned. These focus, of course, on an awareness of our own limitations and continuing presence of our defects of character. People often quote the Step 10 motto, "Be your own harshest critic, and everyone else's most lenient." The Big Book summarizes a similar ethos: "Continue to watch for selfishness, dishonesty, resentment, and fear. When these crop up, we ask God at once to remove them. We discuss them with someone immediately and make amends quickly if we have harmed anyone" (84).

We have already seen how the crucial ingredient of desperation enables miraculous things to happen. The Step 10 experience often involves discovering the proportional lack of perseverance that accompanies "good times." When things are good, people tend to not work the Steps with as much regularity. They do not take inventory as diligently or pray as often. The Big Book is wise to warn us about this: "It is easy to let up the spiritual program and rest on our laurels. We are headed for trouble if we do" (85). But the good news of Step 10 is that when you need them, the Twelve Steps will still be there to be used. There is nothing we can throw at them that they cannot handle.

Spiritual Progress in the Church and AA: Linear or Cyclical?

The reason why people continue working the steps over and over again has to do with AA's understanding that spiritual progress is a cyclical phenomenon rather than a linear one, an understanding which is somewhat atypical. The ever-booming self-help genre of books, for instance, promises fast, easy fixes to many of life's problems. Popular titles like *The Seven Habits of Highly Effective People* suggest that making ourselves over is as easy as reading a book and simply changing our behavior on the basis of it. This would reflect a linear understanding of progress: we move up and up in a straight line, becoming more disciplined, successful, or "effective", improvement being the touchstone of any fulfilling life.

Despite traditional Christian literature's skepticism about self-help, in practice the idea of linear progress has also permeated many Christian churches. Too many churches seem to spend their time emphasizing a check-list series of behaviors that need to be put into practice for growth to occur. Their "teachings" are entirely dominated by moral exhortation and platitudes, only punctuated occasionally with any form of comfort or sensitivity to the realities of daily struggle in the Christian life. As Christian author Michael Horton put it, "we are getting dangerously close to the place in everyday American church life where... Jesus Christ is a coach with a good game plan for our victory rather than a Savior who has already achieved it for us.[86] In effect, these churches are dominated by what the Bible calls "Law", which is shorthand for any form of moral or ethical demand.[87]

While the encouraged habits may be desirable, AA would claim that they are not necessarily achievable through the individual's effort and willpower, regardless of whether a not a person has a serious relationship with God. You might say that AA suspects human nature to be naturally regressive; we lapse just as much in matters of spirituality as we do in New Year's resolutions. Spiritual progress, or sanctification, viewed through the lens of Step 10, is therefore cyclical: we are bound to struggle

---

[86] Michael Horton, *Christless Christianity: the Alternative Gospel of the American Church* (Grand Rapids, MI: Baker Books, 2008), 19. For more on this train of thought, see Mark Galli's "Why We Need More 'Chaplains' and Fewer Leaders" in *Christianity Today*, December 2011.

[87] One of the things that most perturbed Jesus about the church leaders of his time was that they shaped church life in this same way. In Matthew 24, he criticized the Pharisees, saying, "They tie up heavy, cumbersome loads and put them on other people's shoulders, but they themselves are not willing to lift a finger to move them."

with sin again and again, in spite of our best efforts and desires not to. The main thing that discernibly grows in the experience of coming to know God better is one's dependence upon Him and the knowledge of our need for grace.

Because the struggles of life remain essentially the same for the sober *and* drinking alcoholic, there is little stratification between the members of a recovery group; both the 25-year sober drunk and the 5-day sober drunk need the same thing, which is the gift of sobriety, God's gracious gift of reprieve. From the outside looking in, then, AA would appear to have a more pessimistic view of the spiritual life than most Christians are typically willing to acknowledge. AA seems to embrace a more one-way, or monergistic, view of God's work in the life of a believer. Another one of AA's classic sayings is: "Of myself I am nothing, the Father doeth the work."

Theologically speaking, this means that those who hold a more optimistic view of human agency and sanctification over time tend to emphasize moral living, unintentionally downplaying grace. In practice, a heightened understanding of human capability renders the need for grace irrelevant. This has an important implication for how we view others: if you think people have the option to choose differently, then, when they make bad choices, it will be very difficult to have compassion for them.[88]

Does the idea of cyclical sanctification deny that people really do change on account of spirituality? It doesn't; AA is one of the most lucid examples of the exact sort of change that many churches like to advocate. But the results are achieved through an

---

[88] Paul Zahl puts it this way in his book *Grace in Practice:* "One of the reasons we need to embrace the fact of the un-free will is for the sake of its effect on love. A benefit of the un-free will is that it increases mercy in daily relationships and decreases judgment…Forms of Christianity that stress free will create refugees. They get into the business of judging, and especially of judging Christians… Ironically, it is judgment – the absence of it – which drew people to Christ" (108-9).

entirely different set of emphases. Rather than emphasizing growth, a lack of growth is highlighted. Rather than worry about virtue, the pitfalls of self-involvement are decried. For these reasons, we would hesitate to call sanctification "progress" in the moving-forward sense.

Instead, alcoholics in AA are simply sober by the grace of God. The person considered to have the longest-running sobriety of anyone in an AA meeting is whoever woke up earliest that day. If there is indeed anything we can do to keep ourselves sober, it's working the steps – and even our desire to do that relies on the crucial ingredient of desperation. We have already seen how, in the program, our only contribution to spirituality lies is examining our sinfulness, character defects, and reluctance to change. As some fans of the Reformation are quick to say, "we bring nothing to the table but our sin." The rest is left up to God, while we continue working the steps again and again. With this foundation, change happens of its own accord. Indeed, the Big Book promises it.[89]

The 10th Step Promises

While the 9th Step "promises" are more well-known in the world of AA, the Big Book describes another set of promises related to Step 10:

> "And we have ceased fighting anything or anyone – even alcohol. For by this time sanity will have returned. We will seldom be interested in liquor. If tempted, we recoil from it as from a hot flame. *We react sanely and*

---

[89] Lutheran theologian Mark Mattes elaborates a Christian expression of this AA idea: "To be sanctified is to acknowledge God's glory in his imputation… Hence, sanctification is not the goal of the Christian life but its source" (71).

normally, and we will find that this has happened automatically. We will see that our new attitude toward liquor has been given us without any thought or effort on our part. It just comes! That is the miracle of it." (84-86)

It may seem that this passage is primarily concerned with alcohol, but the ramifications are more far reaching. Indeed, what's being described here is the way that growth and transformation actually occur. As we make peace with our past, our future is transformed. The changes that need to happen do so almost entirely of themselves. Life becomes smoothed-over, almost of its own accord. "Automatically" is the word the Big Book uses.

Notice how different this is from most self-help thinking about personal improvement. There are no real goals. The rational mind is not consulted in these considerations. It is put in charge of the back of the bus, since that's where it's understood to have been living the entire time leading up to that point anyway.[90] The person we are to become barely enters into the discussion. That side of things is left up to God. But that's also the fun of it – the adventure comes with trusting God with both our lives and the lives of others. And is it not better that changes should happen this way? Our only alternative involves changing through our own effort and control, and we've seen in Step 1 how well *that* worked! This is a creative enterprise.

Years ago, my sponsor told me something that I will never forget. As I grew more discouraged about giving up smoking, he told me, "When it's time, the cigarettes will just slip away, John." I wondered how I could ever stop without trying to quit, but then I also remembered how many times I *had tried* to quit. So it is with the removal of character defects. Along these lines, Dr. Tiebout offers another piercing insight:

---

[90] An old Christian proverb: "What the heart desires, the will chooses, and the mind justifies."

"Those who view the prospect of *life without abundant drive* as unutterably dull and boring should examine the life of members of Alcoholics Anonymous who have truly adopted the A.A. program. They will see people who have been stopped – and who, therefore, do not have to go anywhere – but people who are learning, for the first time in their lives, to live. They are neither dull nor wishy-washy. Quite the contrary, they are alive and interested in the realities about them. They see things in the large, are tolerant, open-minded, not close-minded bulling ahead. They are receptive to the wonders in the world about them, including the presence of a Deity who makes all this possible. They are the ones who are really living. The attainment of such a way of life is no mean accomplishment."[91]

One Day at a Time

"One day at a time forces you to reckon with the instant you actually occupy, rather than living in fantasy la-la that never arrives."
-Mary Karr, Lit (208)

Alcoholics have often noted how the Big Book discusses what we are to do at the end of the day in Step 10 before it discusses the way we begin the day in Step 11. It's as though looking back takes precedent over looking forward. This is indeed the case with the Twelve Steps, and it operates on the insight that if we wish to have a bright future, we must deal with the past on a daily basis. Such reconciliation allows us to live in the present and leave the future up to its own devices. In other words, without Step 10, Step 11 is relatively useless.

---

[91] Harry Tiebout, "The Ego Factors of Surrender in Alcoholism."

This dynamic plays out perhaps most evidently in a counseling setting. As a minister, I've learned that when a person comes into my office to discuss something important, it is almost impossible to do so until we have first done some catching up. Consequently, I always begin a session by asking, "So what's happened since we last met?" or even, "How was your day?" By answering this question, which involves revisiting the recent past, the subject actually prepares himself to consider the future. Until he has brought himself up to speed with where he is and how he has gotten there, he cannot engage well with where he or I or God would have him go. The answer to my question is not important; the catching up is.

For this reason, "one day at a time" has become arguably AA's most famous slogan. It oozes insight, especially for people who are dealing with hardship and confusion. The future is an abstraction, and AA knows it.

I remember a Christian who entered the rooms of AA. He was frustrated with how he would ever "figure out God's will" for his life if he took things "one day at a time." The two ideas seemed to be at odds with each other. Then a savvy old-timer asked him if he had a relatively clear idea about what the rest of the day would require of him. The newcomer said he did and rattled of a list of a few errands, a meal, a phone call, and some TV before bed. The old-timer responded, "Then you know what God's will is for you." In AA, the future unfolds in twenty-four hour increments. And in my experience, the stories relayed in each AA meeting blow even "the best laid plans of men" out of the water! God's will certainly does unfold, and often in an awe-inspiring fashion, in the life of sober alcoholics. AAs often say that "history ends at midnight." Even if this is not true, Step 10 encourages us to pretend that is.

We will approach tomorrow morning – which means "the future" – in Step 11. Before we do, let's dwell for one more moment on the importance of looking back, with the help of a few words from a man who had little concern for his own safety and future:

> "If you are offering your gift at the altar and there remember that your brother or sister has something against you, leave your gift there in front of the altar. First go and be reconciled to them; then come and offer your gift…do not worry about tomorrow, for tomorrow will worry about itself." (Matt 5: 23-24, 6:34)

Step 11

"Sought through Prayer and Meditation to Improve Our Conscious Contact with God As We Understood Him."

"We constantly remind ourselves that we are no longer running the show, humbly saying to ourselves many times each day 'Thy will be done.' We are then in much less danger of excitement, fear, anger, worry, self-pity, or foolish decisions. We become much more efficient. We do not tire so easily, for we are not burning up energy foolishly as we did when we were trying to arrange life to suit ourselves."
-*Big Book (87-88)*

There's a tale of two lumberjacks from the Pacific Northwest who were cutting timber in Oregon.[92] In that neck of the woods, the older of the two was regarded as the greatest lumberjack that had ever lived. Everyone in the region knew of his famed ability with

---

[92] I first heard a version of this story in a sermon by minister Tony Evans.

an axe. We'll call him Yoda. But there came a time, toward the end of Yoda's life, when a young upstart named Conan started receiving extraordinary acclaim for his stamina, brute strength, and tree-cutting speed.

Eventually, Conan got tired of living in the shadow of Yoda's fame, so he challenged Yoda to a contest to see who could cut down more trees in three days. The winner would, without a doubt, be the greatest lumberjack of all time. After a lot of pressure, Yoda finally accepted the challenge.

The day of the competition soon arrived, and when the starting gun went off, both men started chopping at a furious rate. After an hour or so, Conan noticed from afar that Yoda was taking a brief break, sitting on a stump for five minutes before resuming work. "The old man is washed up", Conan thought to himself, all the while continuing to chop. An hour later, the same thing happened: Yoda stopped chopping and took a little break before returning to the fray. The next hour, the same thing, and so on. Soon Conan was confident that he would surpass his rival's tree count.

At the end of the three days, a judge calculated the number of trees felled by each lumberjack. To Conan's complete surprise, Yoda had cut down twice as many trees as Conan. He approached the old man and asked, "I don't understand. I'm younger than you. I'm stronger than you. I chopped more than you. And you took all those breaks! How did you cut down so many more trees than me?"

Yoda replied, "Every time I paused, I sharpened my axe. After a while, only one of us was chopping with a sharp axe."

Step 11 is the Twelve Steps' way of teaching us to "sharpen our spiritual axe." You know your axe isn't sharp if you notice one day that your car, your wife, your job, and your house aren't nice enough anymore. Working Step 11 saves us a lot of money and heartache, and it usually transforms a bad car into a fine one, a difficult relationship into an easily improved one, and a bad job into "the place where God needs you."

Prayer and Meditation

To stick with the metaphor, the primary stones we use to sharpen our axe are prayer and meditation. Hopefully by the time we get to Step 11, we should already have quite a bit of experience with its inner workings. Indeed, it is impossible to work the first ten steps without doing at least a little bit of praying. But even outside of the Twelve Steps, people who didn't grow up in a religious home may have had experience praying for a grandparent in the hospital, talking to God at a summer camp, or crying to God (i.e. "if you're out there…") alone at the foot of the bed in certain low moments.

Step 11 also mentions meditation. Though the two are quite similar, many have found it helpful to think of prayer as "talking to God" and meditation as "listening to God." Meditation may be more commonly associated with Eastern religions, but the Judeo-Christian tradition also boasts a rich history of meditative practice. In essence, Step 11 involves any vehicle or practice geared toward spiritual growth or deepening. This deepening both improves our perspective and reminds us of our continual dependence on God. For those who have found more contemplative meditation to be frustratingly boring, difficult, or un-engaging, reading and reflecting upon a bit of scripture is a perfectly legitimate option here.[93] But reading the Bible, in this context, has less to do with studying it and more to do with contemplating its implications for

---

[93] Likewise, there are heaps of daily devotional books out there. A couple favorites include the forthcoming *Mockingbird Devotional* and Bo Giertz's *To Live with Christ*. Many people read a page of the *Big Book* every day or night.

one's life. A wise Christian once said that "We don't read the Bible; the Bible reads us."[94]

While some suggest that you *must* have a devotional time every morning to live an actively spiritual life, we simply encourage people to do it whenever they can. "We are not saints. The point is that we are willing to grow along spiritual lines" (84). In fact, it's astonishing how many members of AA talk about working their 11th Step in the morning while sitting in a stall in the bathroom at work. That's okay too. "It works – it really does…We found that God does not make too hard terms with those who seek Him" (88, 46). Another important avenue for the 11th Step is church involvement, which supplements individual spiritual practices with the vital element of group fellowship.

My favorite old-timer, Chuck T., was known for asking his sponsees about their 11th Step practice at the oddest moments. He would receive a phone call from an anxious sponsee, seeking advice about some situation involving a girlfriend or a co-worker. After hearing him out, and without in any way addressing the phone call's main concern, he would ask, "What book are you reading at the moment?" "But Chuck, didn't you hear what I said she did?!" "Yes, I heard you", he would respond, "and I asked you what spiritual book are you reading at the moment?"[95]

Without being at all legalistic, we must admit that we regret when the practice of Step 11 falls out of our daily routines. To use

---

[94] This "charismatic" approach to reading the Bible contrasts with some Christian ideas that demand precise, academic methods, for fear of someone misinterpreting the Bible. The person who has reached Step 11 will be quick to question the selfish motives that might warp his reading. In spite of Luther's insistence that "when the enthusiast reads the Bible, all he sees are his own dreams", we still believe it is important to consider Scripture through the lens of its personal impact, as though it were a "living word" – written fresh for the reader each morning and designed, in part, to illuminate or speak to some aspect of her life.

[95] Here is a list of some of my favorite Step 11-related books: The Bible (NIV, ESV, or NRSV) and the Mockingbird list, which can be found online at: http://www.mbird.com/2011/04/2011-nyc-conference-book-table/

an image from the *12 & 12*, Step 11 functions in a human being's life the way sunlight does to a plant. It offers us time to connect with the source of our being and the One who knows all that we need. Chuck's pointed question draws attention to the helpfulness of daily Step 11 practice. When it's combined with the daily practice of Step 10, a profoundly practical spiritual life blossoms:

> "There is a direct linkage among self-examination, meditation, and prayer. Taken separately, these practices can bring much relief and benefit. But when they are logically related and interwoven, the result is an unshakable foundation for life. Now and then we may be granted a glimpse of that ultimate reality which is God's kingdom." (*12 & 12*, 98)

Experimenting with Prayer: "Pick a Card"

"In thinking about our day we may face indecision. We may not be able to determine which course to take. Here we ask God for inspiration, an intuitive thought or a decision. We relax and take it easy. We don't struggle. We are often surprised how the right answers come after we have tried this for a while."
-Big Book (86)

"God's office is at the end of your rope."
-Unknown

The *12 & 12* encourages imagination in our prayer lives. Prayer opens us up to possibilities. Prayer tears down the walls of the ego. It takes us from the place of hubris to the place of humility. It puts our lives back in the hands that can handle them. For this reason, the practice of Step 11 feels quite natural once we begin to do it.

Those of us who have come to make use of it cannot imagine going back to a life without prayer.[96]

Again, like the rest of the Steps, Step 11 encourages a person to yield passively to God's activity. [97] One practical way to approach Step 11 in this way is via a so-called "prayer experiment." For example, you might consider a situation in your life with which you are not pleased. Do any of your current circumstances or relationships cause you anxiety? "Pick a card, any card." Whatever issue comes to mind will be the topic of your prayer experiment.

Usually we experience anxiety in a situation to the exact extent that our "activity" has failed to solve our problem. Can you not conclude that you have tried to fix the situation on your own? Have you not exerted yourself in an attempt to change it? People usually don't get to the point of needing Step 11 until their efforts have failed them. We might say that *faith begins at the point where your individual power ends*.

With a topic in mind, the prayer experiment hopefully enables us to cease in our attempts to bring about a particular outcome. We agree to pray every day for thirty days about the situation, doing our best to trust God to deal with the situation *for* us. If we have an understanding friend whom we can tell about

---

[96] See also: Aaron Zimmerman's "boulder-carrying" story quoted in Step 3, in the section entitled "True Mysticism: Life in Reality."

[97] The inspiration for this principle originally came from the Reformational distinction between *passive* and *active righteousness*. Martin Luther drew this distinction in his famous *Commentary on Galatians*. He suggested that the world is obsessed with what he called "active righteousness." The idea is that human activity is the force that creates breakthroughs in life, and the contemporary expressions of it are commonplace terms like "being pro-active" and "Type A." In contrast, Luther suggested that where the spiritual life is concerned, passivity is actually more important than activity. Passivity yields to God, while activity often shuts Him out. Thus, he said, for the Christian who puts their faith in Christ, God confers upon them "passive righteousness." Step 11 affirms the importance of passivity in the spiritual life.

this new prayer topic at the outset, we should. It will be exciting for that friend to see what, if anything, happens. After 30 days of praying, we discuss the results with our friend. We might even touch base with our friend on a weekly basis to see if anything fresh unfolds. In almost every instance, this approach yields far better results and far more change than the alternative (and more intuitive) method of asserting our willpower to get what we want. By taking our hands off the wheel, we end up treating God like he is, indeed, God.

A common Christian maxim says that "We are the only hands and feet that God has on Earth." While these words may sound profound, the prayer experiment approach assumes the exact opposite about God: *we are not God's hand and feet; God is very capable of working upon a situation without our being involved in the fixing of it.* We treat God like He has His own hands, thank you very much. Christians call these spiritual appendages of their higher power the Holy Spirit. Prayer experiments are our attempts to give God more credit and ourselves less, acknowledging that His work in our lives is creative and not contrived. "Let go and let God" is the classic AA way of saying this.

Consider an example of this approach, which involves my friend Benson and his fiancé, whom we'll call Harriet. Benson and Harriet fell madly in love. After a year of dating they eagerly got engaged to be married. This all occurred at a time when the economy was taking a nosedive, and just a few months into their relationship, Harriet lost her job working at an architecture firm. Fortunately, her parents were able to help provide for her needs as she began to look for a new job.

Fast forward to the beginning of their engagement, when Benson came to the church for a pastoral visit. Benson was concerned that Harriet was not very motivated about her job hunt. He was about to start a teaching career, and worried that she would soon become frustrated by his inability to provide her with a lifestyle comparable to the one she had experienced growing up. He did not want to marry a girl who didn't want to work, especially if he thought she would be disappointed with (or resent) his financial means.

Unfortunately for Harriet, Benson soon started trying to motivate her to find a job himself. He would ask her how many resumes she had sent out at the end of a work day. "Have you called that place back to follow up?" If Benson didn't like Harriet's answers or felt that she hadn't done "enough", he would treat her somewhat coldly, withholding love until he felt she had earned it from him in her job hunt. Not only did she have to deal with unemployment on her own time, now she had to put up with Benson's passive-aggression as well. Poor girl! Needless to say, she had withdrawn a bit too, always careful to dodge certain topics, lest they prompt yet another uncomfortable exchange about her job search.

I suggested that Benson try a prayer experiment. He agreed to start his morning each day with a prayer that he be given the ability to trust God with Harriet's job search. Benson tried his best to avoid the topic unless she brought it up, at which point he would listen and only offer advice if it was asked for. He kept me abreast of any progress. Initially, the status of Harriet's job search remained the same, but Benson reported that he felt differently about it.

After about a month, Harriet did something that surprised Benson: she applied for a job at a local supermarket. It impressed him that she valued the simple importance of bringing home a paycheck, even if the job wasn't glamorous. He was excited to relay that she had done this of her own volition, and that he had been able to tell her how great he thought it was. I thought it was great too.

Then a few weeks later, she also found a part-time job teaching tennis lessons. Suddenly Harriet was working two jobs.

Benson was impressed. We decided the experiment was working so well that it should be continued for another month.

One day, while Harriet was working at the supermarket, something happened. A former co-worker from an architecture firm came into the supermarket. Harriet had to check her out and, as they made small talk, the fact that she had not been able to find another job in their field came up. Needless to say, Harriet felt humiliated. When Benson picked her up from work that evening, she burst into tears in the car. He was able to be incredibly affirming and sweet. It gave him an opportunity to tell Harriet how much he respected her willingness to humble herself for the sake of bringing in an income, in spite of the fact that her parents were willing to support her financially. He told her that what he saw in her was much more important than an impressive job; she had character and backbone. That's why he wanted to marry her, and not the girl from the check-out line. It was a tender moment.

And then a few weeks later, Harriet got another – a third! – part-time job working in an architecture office, working a job more in line with her graduate school training. Benson reported, first and foremost, that she was happy. He couldn't believe how dimwitted he had been, thinking she wasn't capable of finding a job. God had taught Benson that Harriet was capable of working harder than him, holding down three jobs simultaneously. By the time their wedding day arrived, Benson was convinced that he was the luckier of the two parties being joined together as one. He knew without a shadow of a doubt that he could trust God with her in such a way that he could focus his attention on being a supportive spouse and ally, instead of a critical parental voice. What's more, the whole experience had brought them closer together and taught them how to lean on each other in times of difficulty. They were ready and excited to spend their lives together.

All this to say, we prefer passive spirituality to active spirituality any day of the week!

The Difference between God and Santa Claus

"Although we have a 'merit badge' mentality, prayer shows us that we are actually 'punished' by any expectation of merit and reward."
-Richard Rohr

The Big Book offers an important word of warning about Step 11 and the possibility for selfishness that prayer sometimes brings:

> "We ask especially for freedom from self-will, and are careful to make no request for ourselves only. We may ask for ourselves, however, if others will be helped. *We are careful never to pray for our own selfish ends.* Many of us have wasted a lot of time doing that and it doesn't work." (87)

Here we encounter the difference between God and Santa Claus. Prayerful petitions are not the same thing as a child's Christmas list. As we have mentioned, God's will and our own often find themselves at odds with each other. We are rarely inclined to ask for the right thing from God, and we do well to realize that God can answer a prayer in many different ways: "yes", "no", and "...later" are all options. Step 11 is the Step that shows us how these should be our answers for ourselves as well. "At no time had we asked what God's will was for us; instead we had been telling Him what it ought to be" (*12 & 12,* 31). The Reverend R-J Heijmen eloquently points out the implication of this disconnect between self-interest and (true) spirituality:

> "In our constant quest for happiness, for peace, the answer is to be found not in the quest for control, but in the release of it…As we walk through life, constantly frustrated by our inability to be and do what we want, the answer is not self-mastery, but rather the love of the Master."[98]

Step 11 is where we begin to realize both that prayer typically changes us more than it changes God, and that this truth is actually good news. The Big Book's necessary reproof against self-centered prayer has been known to lead AAs far afield from ever praying about anything specific for fear that they will infect the prayer with their own self-centeredness. Just like impure motives for amends-making or Bible reading, AA understands selfishness in the arena of prayer to be unavoidable. At the same time, however, some of our motives for praying will be good, and God can use the bad ones too. If we had to have pure motives to engage in spiritual practices, no one could ever seek a higher power in the first place.[99]

Despite the danger of selfishness, therefore, we believe that *praying about specific situations is a good thing*. Praying out loud and with other people at appropriate times is an important and helpful skill that many of us are glad to offer and use. The classic "…if it be Thy will" tag line, far from a pious rejoinder, can be a useful suffix for any particular concern.

---

[98] Heijmen, R-J, entry in the *Mockingbird Devotional*, Ed. Ethan Richardson (Charlottesville, VA: Mockingbird, forthcoming).
[99] Christianity also affirms God's ability to work through humans with impure motives. Three books of the Old Testament were ascribed to Solomon, an ancestor of Jesus, who was born as a result of King David committing adultery and murder. Similarly, the New Testament authors take great care to show how Peter, the founder of the Christian Church, had consistent failures as a disciple and a church leader. Again, God works through human limitations.

One of my favorite personal examples of Step 11 impact comes from when I first graduated from college. I had a girlfriend with whom I was quite infatuated, too much so in fact. In a sense she had become my god, the source of my security and hope for the future. I had come to need her affirmation too much, and not surprisingly, she began to withdraw. Like many men before me, I tried all kinds of ploys to keep her interested. But the more I became dependent upon her, the more I actually chased her away. It's no wonder. After all, who could possibly handle the responsibility of being another person's god?

When all of my attempts to keep the relationship going had run out of steam, I finally turned to Step 11. For the first time in years, I prayed a specific, on my knees, out-loud and heartfelt prayer: *"God, please don't let her leave me. I'll do anything!"*

I believe that God heard my prayer clearly that day…and then she dumped me! At the time, I felt like a part of my very being had been amputated. I later came to appreciate the seemingly callous words that my friend Nick had offered me at the time: "One day you'll thank God that you didn't marry that girl."

It wasn't long afterward that I found myself in an Episcopal church service of Morning Prayer for the first time in years. We opened our prayer books and recited the classic words of confession that I hadn't heard since my youth: *"We have erred and strayed from Thy ways like lost sheep. We have followed too much the devices and desires of our own hearts."* That moment was the beginning my return to church, which eventually led me to the ministry.

Perhaps even more importantly, these experiences paved the way for the day that would come three years later in Brooklyn, when I met my wife for the first time and fell in love in a way that I had never dreamed possible.

Bearing all this in mind, here are two suggestions about how to pray: First, don't be afraid to begin with the words, "Thank you for _____" Second, consider completing the sentence, "Dear

Lord, today I need your help with _____." Such prayer helps us to keep the emphasis on God's ability to use us, rather than on our desire to use Him.

On A Personal Note

As a longtime member of AA, I'm convinced that Christianity offers an enormous amount to people in recovery. For me, Christianity has been a deepening of the things I learned from the Twelve Steps about human nature and God.

Lest we forget, in Step 11 the Church's contributions are welcomed and encouraged. The Big Book reminds us to "Be quick to see where religious people are right" (87). A crucial way for alcoholics to pursue their spiritual lives is through the fellowship and the massive theological resources of organized religion. But it takes some time for the new member of AA to reach that point; rarely will a person in the first six months of sobriety be ready to re-connect with the Church.

It's unfortunate that the Christian Church often gets frustrated with AA for not beginning the Twelve Steps with Step 11. They fail to realize that AA is so effective precisely *because* it starts with the problem and not with the solution. Martin Luther famously claimed that an awareness of sin always precedes a person's ability to hear the good news of Christianity, that the thirst must come before the drink, that the Gospel follows the Law. In a similar fashion, the alcoholic will not find sobriety until he cannot stay sober. Surrender presupposes a lost battle. So we must caution Christians who want to make Step 11 into Step 1 and Step 1 into Step 2. Rushing the newly sober person to church does not benefit anyone.

On the other hand, we find that many who have encountered this message of God's grace in AA soon start coming to church of their own accord. They have the hard-won ability to read the Bible with fresh eyes. My own congregation contains many people who have returned to the Christian faith after three, four and five years sober, because "now it all makes sense in a way that it never did before." Their enthusiasm is inspiring. Whenever recovering addicts start showing up at a particular church, it's an encouraging sign that the church is keyed in to the message of God's grace.

Step 12

"Having Had a Spiritual Awakening as the Result of These Steps, We Tried to Carry this Message to Alcoholics, and to Practice These Principles in All Our Affairs."

"But obviously you cannot transmit something you haven't got."
-*Big Book (164)*

"To progress is to begin again."
-*Martin Luther*

The recovery and sense of peace that AAs often experience after completing the first eleven steps naturally makes them want to share them with others – this was Bill Wilson's motivation behind the program in the first place. Step 12 makes such outreach official, providing yet another important means for us to focus, in a life-long capacity, on our usefulness to others. In fact, far from being an epilogue to recovery, Step 12 is as integral a part of the program as the eleven Steps that precede it. It is useful to divide this step into several parts: *1)* "Having had a spiritual awakening as the result of these steps", *2)* "we tried to carry this message to alcoholics", and *3)* "to practice these principles in all our affairs." We'll discuss them in back-to-front order, beginning with the third.

Part 3 – "We Tried... to Practice These Principles in All Our Affairs.

In a general sense, this third part refers to the importance of continuing to practice the first 11 Steps. They never get old. There is nothing life can throw at us that they won't enable us to deal with. "Third verse, same as the first" (Violent Femmes) .

The first 11 Steps follow a single guiding principle, summarized by the well-known AA slogan: "honesty is the best policy." Love may be the highest virtue for most people, but in AA two other virtues receive a similar elevation. These are honesty and humility. Perhaps these two virtues are so acclaimed in the world of sobriety because addicts are so familiar with their opposites – dishonesty and egotism. Honesty in particular provides the foundation for part three of Step 12's reiteration of the first 11 Steps.

AA teaches that the person who is incapable of being (rigorously) honest is also incapable of staying sober. The Big Book says this in very frank terms in a famous passage which is read, almost liturgically, at the beginning of most AA meetings:

> "Those who do not recover are people who cannot or will not completely give themselves to this simple program, usually men and women who are constitutionally incapable of being honest with

themselves. There are such unfortunates. They are not at fault; they seem to have been born that way. *They are naturally incapable of grasping and developing a manner of living which demands rigorous honestly.* There are those too, who suffer from grave emotional and mental disorders, but many of them do recover if they have the capacity to be honest." (60)

The Twelve Steps require honesty, even though it's often easier said than done. Indeed, like all virtue, honesty is a gift from God that cannot be inwardly generated. In the same way that water—while capable of boiling—cannot heat itself, you and I may be capable of being honest but we cannot make ourselves so. For this reason the Twelve Steps are shaped in such a way that they invoke honesty, thereby inspiring either acquiescence or flight. People simply do not work the Steps dishonestly – it would be an oxymoron. If they cannot keep from being dishonest, they will balk at some crucial point, usually in the middle of Steps 4 and 5 or just before they get to Step 9. Consider the words of the Big Book:

> "Time after time newcomers have tried to keep to themselves certain facts about their lives. Trying to avoid this humbling experience, they have turned to easier methods [i.e., ones that don't require 'rigorous honesty']. Almost invariably they got drunk…they had not learned enough of humility, fearlessness and honesty, in the sense we find it necessary…" (72-73)

While we are skeptical about the helpfulness of exhortation and the efficacy of "speaking the truth in love" for the alcoholic, we must acknowledge that secrets are very dangerous. "You're only as sick as your secrets," goes the maxim, and most alcoholics have lived lives that were deeply enshrouded in deceit and manipulation.

In the context of recovery, too much honesty is far preferable to not enough of it.

In fact, as far as Twelve Step spirituality is concerned, it is impossible to love effectively without honesty and humility. You could say we need to *"get* straight before we can *give* straight." We get straight through the working of Steps 1 through 11, which requires no small measure of honesty.

As we've noted, desperation may be the only thing that can produce the spiritual fuel needed to work the steps. The Christian who understands this dynamic might say that we cannot repent unless the Holy Spirit quickens the human heart. If we are not aware of our shortcomings, we will not be able to identify with others in the midst of their suffering. And if we cannot empathize with others, we will not be able to love them. As long as we remain incapable of being honest, therefore, we will remain incapable of loving.

Part 2 – "...We Tried to Carry This Message to Alcoholics..."

"You've got to give it away to keep it."
-AA slogan

It is important to note that the original version of Step 12 read slightly differently: "We tried to carry this message to other *people*", not "other alcoholics." So when AAs talk about "doing 12th Step work", they are usually referring to an act of charity, designed to benefit a person other than the one making the effort. It may involve something as meaningful as leading people through the Twelve Steps as a sponsor, or as thankless as cleaning ash trays before meetings. It will probably involve drinking a lot of coffee.

Maybe it means taking a guy out to breakfast before a morning AA meeting. The Big Book paints an even more dramatic picture:

> "Helping others is the foundation stone of your recovery. You have to act the Good Samaritan every day, if need be. It may mean the loss of many nights' sleep, great interference with your pleasures, interruptions to your business. It may mean sharing your money and your home, counseling frantic wives and relatives, innumerable trips to police courts, sanitariums, hospitals, jails and asylums. Your telephone may jangle at any time of the day or night. Your wife may sometimes say she is neglected. A drunk may smash the furniture in your home, or burn a mattress. You may have to fight with him if he becomes violent. Sometimes you will have to call a doctor and administer sedatives under his direction. Another time you may have to send for the police or an ambulance. Occasionally you will have to meet such conditions." (97)

Remember Jesus' "blessed are the meek" line from the Sermon on the Mount? The Twelve Steps agree. The driving virtue behind this crucial aspect of life, "being of service", is humility. I recently overheard someone saying, "I've become convinced that nothing matters more in this life than confidence." It's a view that epitomizes the opposite of AA's standpoint. In Twelve Step spirituality, humility is king. Many AAs think of it this way: *helping another person will help you more than anything you can possibly do for yourself.*

Because AA holds humility in such high esteem, people in recovery spend a lot of time finding ways to serve other people. You could say they seek out opportunities to be selfless for selfish reasons. A short throw-away line in the Big Book makes this clear:

"If sex is very troublesome, we throw ourselves the harder into helping others. We think of their needs and work for them. This takes us out of ourselves" (70). It may sound contrived or disingenuous, but the results of this outward focus quickly change one's attitude toward it. Even if the initial gesture feels fake or forced, the attendant happiness is often transformative, not to mention alluring.

This leads into another, now-familiar AA motif that real virtue is born of necessity – we help others because it keeps us sober. We do not become sober and then move to a position of service; instead, the two are inextricable. The newest member of AA is capable of and benefits from service work. This is another AA insight that Christians may find helpful in an environment that too often divorces personal spiritual 'recovery' from service to others. Some of the perceptions of self-righteousness in the Christian Church may derive from its focus on service as something that strong, spiritually 'mature' people do with their newfound spiritual resources of virtue and strength of will, rather than the work of the weak and needy themselves.

If people in AA didn't find that being helpful made them happier than any other alternatives, they would have stopped doing it in the 1940s. Instead, AA has become a beacon of tangible hope, in part because of its allegiance to the importance of humility.

Humility: Three Stories

"Practical experience shows that nothing will so much insure immunity from drinking as intensive work with other alcoholics. It works when other activities fail. This is our twelfth suggestion: Carry this message to other alcoholics!...Life will take on new meaning."
-Big Book (89)

No more important example of the 12th Step ever occurred than the one in Akron, Ohio in early June of 1935. A sober alcoholic who had recently become sold on the Twelve Steps found himself on a business trip and in jeopardy of falling off the wagon once again. He came to believe that the most effective way for him to remain sober was to carry his message to another alcoholic.

At first, a string of clergymen refused to let him contact any of the alcoholics in their congregations, fearing that the only thing worse than one alcoholic is two. But they were wrong, thank God. Eventually he was put in touch with a local doctor who also had a notorious substance-abuse problem. He called the number only to find that the poor doctor was currently passed out under his kitchen table, but that they could meet up the next afternoon.

So Dr. Bob reluctantly walked into an awkward encounter with a complete stranger, thanks in large part to his wife's prodding. He led with the line, "I don't think you can help me with my drinking problem." Bill Wilson then responded with the famous words: *"I'm not here to help you with your drinking, I'm here to help me with mine."* That interchange marked the official birth of AA, and it's a testament to the 12th Step's brilliance. As we've suggested, AA teaches that the best way to sell a person on humility is to appeal to his sense of self-interest. While we don't glorify self-interest, it's such an innate part of the human condition that true humility can only begin once we recognize the selfish character of what often passes for our virtue.

The following story illustrates the same point more concisely. A young man freshly sober, having only recently finished his first eleven steps, sought out a newcomer in a meeting and offered to take him through the Twelve Steps. After only a few interactions, the newcomer went on a binge. The confused young sponsor called his wiser, more experienced sponsor and confessed, "I'm not good at the 12th Step. My sponsee just got drunk." His sponsor promptly replied, "It sounds to me like your

12th Step efforts worked perfectly. *You're* still sober, aren't you? Clearly your work with him did the trick!" That's the AA angle – and it's a good one. Bill writes about this dynamic in his chapter on "Working with Others":

> "Actually, he may be helping you more than you are helping him. Make it plain he is under no obligation to you, that you hope only that he will try to help other alcoholics when he escapes his own difficulties…You should not be offended if he wants to call it off, for he has helped you more than you have helped him." (94)

Perhaps no man in the history of the world has come to understand this principle better than Paul of Tarsus. His epistles that make up much of the New Testament display this otherworldly concern for others in a most striking way. The fact that many of these letters were written from a prison cell speaks volumes. Here was a man who learned to find great joy in the face of extreme difficulty and persecution by focusing on the well-being of others.

One of the most moving portraits of this humility (and its impact on others) comes from the book of Acts. After being "flogged severely" (read: beaten), Paul and his traveling companion, Silas, were thrown into a prison cell for disturbing the peace at a local synagogue in modern-day Turkey:

> About midnight Paul and Silas were praying and singing hymns to God, and the other prisoners were listening to them. Suddenly there was such a violent earthquake that the foundations of the prison were shaken. At once all the prison doors flew open, and everyone's chains came loose. The jailer woke up, and when he saw the prison doors open, he drew his sword and was about to kill

himself because he thought the prisoners had escaped. But Paul shouted, "Don't harm yourself! We are all here!"

The jailer called for lights, rushed in and fell trembling before Paul and Silas. He then brought them out and asked, "Sirs, what must I do to be saved?"

Then they spoke the word of the Lord to him and to all the others in his house. At that hour of the night the jailer took them and washed their wounds; then immediately he and all his household were baptized. The jailer brought them into his house and set a meal before them; he was filled with joy because he had come to believe in God—he and his whole household. (16:23-34)

Notice that Paul's attention is entirely directed toward the other inmates, who were no doubt surprised by the way that Paul and Silas kicked off their prison stay. How could two men, after being beaten and imprisoned, sing songs of praise to God? And Paul's concern for others was clearly striking to the other inmates, who soon became his friends. The author points out that "the other prisoners were listening to them."

The impact that Paul and Silas had upon the other inmates was so great that the others followed their lead when the doors flew open, staying in the cell. The entire group now turned their attention to the jailer, whose life was, according to Paul, more important than leaving the confines of a prison: "Don't harm yourself! We are all here!" The jailer was astonished and immediately embraced a life lived according this new set of concerns. He was converted, in other words, and it is not too much of a stretch to say that a Holy-Spirit driven version of Step 12 inspired him to make the leap from hopeless despair to infectious, deep-seated joy – all in a matter of minutes.

Self-centeredness focuses energy upon only one individual. Humility, by contrast, focuses on everyone but the self. In this passage from Acts, we see Paul's concern was for Silas, then the prisoners, then the jailer, and then the jailer's family. The result was fresh conviction in the goodness and reality of God's grace. Those who came to find it also found "joy", "*because he had come to believe in God—he and his whole household.*"

The Episcopalian evangelist John Burwell describes this dynamic through the image of two Israeli lakes. In the northern part of Israel there is an enormous lake that, in spite of the arid climate, is surrounded by verdant banana plantations. This lake, the Sea of Galilee, is fed from the north by the small Jordan River. At the south end of the lake, the river continues to flow for miles, all the way down to a second lake.

But unlike the first lake, this second one does not have any tributaries leading out from it. All the water that comes into it stagnates and eventually evaporates. That lake is called The Dead Sea, because nothing grows in it.

The first lake gives all it has. The water that comes into it soon flows out. Because of this, the lake is full of large fish and the soil surrounding it is nutrient-rich, ideal for tropical crops. The lake has supported life in the area for thousands of years. Meanwhile, the Dead Sea supports no one. It is a repellent place, visited for the sheer extremity of its buoyancy and desolate atmosphere. "Remember the words the Lord Jesus himself said: 'It is more blessed to give than to receive'" (Acts 20:35). Perhaps his familiarity with these two lakes served as an illustration of this truth.

STEP 12

The Secret to "Carrying the Message"

"You catch more flies with honey than with vinegar."
-Old Southern saying

"Knowledge puffs up, but love builds up."
-1 Corinthians 8:1

The story of old-timer Dick A's first encounter with AA illustrates what it means to "carry the message":

> "So I walked up to the payphone and dialed the number for AA. I started crying, saying, 'I'm an alcoholic.' Instead of rejecting me, she said, 'just a minute, you wait right there' and sent out a guy named Ed.
> ...I actually resisted listening to him for while, because I thought he wasn't hip like me; I knew that I was just down on my luck. Ed, on the other hand, looked like he'd never had any luck in the first place.
> But then I saw his eyes. He did what it talks about in the Big Book: he relived the horrors of his past with me. He told me about himself, and he did something that I learned a great lesson from.
> He asked about me. He said, 'what do you do?', and I started crying. I said, 'I think I'm an alcoholic.' But he cut me off and said, 'No, what did you do for a living before drinking got the better of you?'
> And I told him about my writing. He actually recognized some of the things I'd written, and he said: 'that's great stuff! You're very talented. God must really have something in mind for you.'
> Then I just broke down and started crying, because no one had said anything kind or hopeful to me

in years. And if he hadn't done that, I would not be here sober today.

He had read the Big Book and he understood that we don't get anyone into recovery by being tough on 'em, but we get people here by unconditional love. They're already hurt and they've already been through enough hell. We don't need to add to it. We need to let them know that there's a place where there's hope. And that's what Ed did for me.

After we had talked for a little while, Ed put me into his Pinto to get me something to drink so that he could help me taper off the booze, because I was now starting to vibrate. He realized that I was going into DTs [delerium tremens], because he had worked with wet drunks before. He asked, "Are you going to be okay? I'm going to stop here for just one minute to get some money so we can get you on track." And he got out of the car to use an ATM. It was the first ATM machine I'd ever seen. They were pretty new in 1977.

It was a hot day, June the 8, 1977 in Atlanta. So he goes up to the machine to get his $20 or whatever, and before he can get back to the car, I couldn't get the door open because my hands were rattling so much, and I had thrown up all down the inside of his brand new Pinto. *And the only thing that he did when he opened the door and saw what had happened, was put his arm around me. He said: 'It's going to be okay.' If he had been critical of me, I wouldn't be here tonight.*

But Ed knew that we don't have new cars, new jobs, or new lives unless we're willing to work with another alcoholic, and he loved me and he cared for me and he took me to a place where I could weather the withdrawals."

Dick's story reveals the profound impact that grace has upon people. He is quick to contrast grace with criticism, and the distinction is a helpful one. Encouragement and affirmation are far more powerful in straightening someone out than any amount of advice. The one-way love of grace can accomplish what no amount of criticism can, and it tends to be most effective in the cases where all other attempts to create change have failed, alcoholism being the perfect example.

For this reason, most talk therapy is helpful for someone going through a tough time. Even a totally inexperienced counselor or a novice lay minister can benefit someone who is looking for help. Indeed, the primary impact of therapy does not come from anything the therapist says, but from their affirming and focused presence. The simple power of having someone "in your corner", listening to you, taking an interest in you, entering into your life from the outside and caring, does wonders for a suffering person. [100] The therapist models the nourishing love of God. She embodies the good news of the Gospel – that God desires to help and not to punish the sinner – in a concrete way (John 3:17). We all need it, and most of us have too little experience with encouragement. But we are unable to impart or benefit much from true compassion until we have become aware of our own failings.[101]

---

[100] Stephen Ministry is a great contemporary example of a lay ministry that understands this material implicitly, providing people going through rough times with a Christian friend who will listen and pray, but without any agenda other than helping the person to connect with God in the midst of difficulty.
[101] For the person who doesn't want help, all you can do is highlight the truth as you've seen it play out and then abandon him to the surprisingly effective hand of consequences. 12th Step work originally involved sober alcoholics sharing the reality of their hopeless plight with wet drunks. Many embraced the program of recovery once experience convinced them that the AAs were right about their condition. I saw this play out in an Alabama meeting, where a girl in her twenties shared that she wasn't "sure if I'm an alcoholic or not." An old-timer piped up with a callous but brilliant response: "Well honey, you go back out and do some more drinking. We'll be here

The 12th Step understands the therapeutic insight that in order to help a downcast person, presence is the key. The ability to empathize and affirm are all that is required. Ed gives us a perfect illustration of this reality. Too many people, both in AA and the world at large, believe that troubled people need "advice" and "exhortation" in order to get their life sorted out after a misstep or collapse. As we've noted, people in the last several decades have been leaving Christian churches in droves because of unwanted, demanding, and ultimately ineffective advice, advice which is almost always perceived by the targeted audience as judgment. The truth is that compassion achieves all of these things and more. You'll catch more flies with honey than with vinegar.

Part 1 - "Having Had a Spiritual Awakening as the Result of These Steps"

The first part of Step 12 describes a final, all-encompassing promise. If we work the program, we'll experience a "spiritual awakening." It's impossible to work the Steps fully without experiencing the fruit that accompanies the program. We have already described the various shifts in perspective that constitute such a change, but Bill Wilson's insightful definition of "spiritual awakening" is nevertheless a helpful one:

> "When a man or a woman has a spiritual awakening, the most important meaning of it is that *he has now become able to do, feel, and believe that which he could not do before on his unaided strength and resources alone.* He has been granted a gift which amounts to a new state of consciousness and

---

waiting for you when you get back." Luther called this approach "leading with the law."

being. He has been set on a path which tells him he is really going somewhere, that life is not a dead end, not something to be endured or mastered...He finds himself in possession of a degree of honesty, tolerance, unselfishness, peace of mind, and love of which he had thought himself quite incapable." (*12 &12*, 107)

We hope that people can identify with this description of spiritual life. Do we see things differently than we used to? Has God given us what the famous AA writer Chuck C. described as "a new pair of glasses"? Perhaps we've come to doubt the value of willpower and self-sufficiency. Hopefully we have come to appreciate the sublime importance of weakness and being wrong.

I had to answer these questions in my own life when I decided to go into the ministry. When someone first suggested that I consider becoming a minister, I thought to myself: "No way! I don't want to do that, and God knows I won't do it unless I want to." Two years later, my feelings about that vocation had completely changed. Somehow it had become all I could see myself doing, and I was convinced it was the only job in the world for me. Another friend asked, "Doesn't it bother you that you won't have much control over where you are going to live and work?" He was surprised to hear me say that *that* aspect of becoming a minister – not having to figure out my future for myself – was one of the most attractive features of the job. The loss of control constituted a feeling of relief. It was by far the better of the two options.

In the final section of an essay on Step 12, Bill Wilson described the way that a spiritual awakening reorients a person's perspective on life. It is beautiful portrait of humility, one of the finest passages in all of AA's literature. We wish to close with it:

"Still more wonderful is the feeling that we do not have to be specially distinguished among our fellows in order to be useful and profoundly happy. Not many of us can be leaders of prominence, nor do we wish to be. Service, gladly rendered, obligations squarely met, troubles well accepted or solved with God's help, the knowledge that at home or in the world outside we are partners in a common effort, the well-understood fact that in God's sight all human beings are important, the proof that love freely given surely brings a full return, the certainty that we are no longer isolated and alone in self-constructed prisons, the surety that we need no longer be square pegs in round holes but can fit and belong in God's scheme of things – these are the permanent and legitimate satisfactions of right living for which no amount of pomp and circumstance, no heap of material possessions, could possibly be substitutes. True ambition is not what we thought it was. *True ambition is the deep desire to live usefully and humbly under the grace of God.*" (*12 & 12*, 125)

Conclusion

What the Church Can Learn From Alcoholics Anonymous – and Vice Versa

The ironic and sad truth is that in AA one finds a much better example of Christian community than in many churches. This is a controversial statement, but there is much evidence to support it. AA presents an impressive model for church, not to mention evangelism: it started with two drunks in 1939 and today has almost as many members as the Anglican Communion. The Big Book is one of the best-selling books of all-time, having sold over 30 million copies. How has this happened? Especially when there is nobody saying "we have to grow"? There are no altar calls in AA. A small percentage of people are pushed there by the courts,[102] but most attend because they want to be there. AA, in

---

[102] There's a *South Park* episode dealing with this (Season 9, Episode 14), which, incidentally, I don't recommend.

this sense, is truly phenomenal, having grown far beyond what any of the founders could have envisioned.

Of course, the same could be said of the growth of Christendom with regard to the twelve disciples from Galilee, that they never in their wildest dreams could have imagined the impact their ministry would have upon the world, even 2000 years later. But with AA, the growth is so fresh, unavoidable and seemingly uncontrived. It is no wonder that author Kurt Vonnegut once claimed that America's two greatest contributions to the world were "AA and jazz."[103]

AA as Church: Hospital For Sinners (No Saints Allowed!)

AA is full of people from all walks of life. There are many meetings, for example, where in every gathering, "a bum sits next to a millionaire." In spite of the differences in circumstance, each member is vividly aware of his personal history of failure, demoralization, and weakness.

There are no thrones in AA, no priests, no leaders – only volunteers who wield no more power than the newest member of the group. AA's 2nd Tradition states: "For our group purpose there is but one ultimate authority – a loving God as He may express Himself in our group conscience. Our leaders are but trusted servants; they do not govern." In other words, status is a complete non-starter, institutionally-speaking.

Consequently, AA believes there is no fundamental distinction to be drawn between the message that should be given to newcomers (in Christian terms, non-believers, seekers, and new converts), and mature AAs (members of church leadership and stalwart long-term adherents of the faith). Churches that take this

---

[103] Kurt Vonnegut, "The Work to Be Done", *Rolling Stone*, May 28, 1998.

approach are few and far between. But in AA the same message that saves a drunk can also perform the miraculous trick of sanctifying him (i.e., keeping him saved), no matter how long he has been coming. In other words, the same hope that gets you in, also keeps you in.

This contrasts with a view held by many mainstream churches, namely that the Sunday message for Christians should be different from the message for non-believers. In other words, many churches act on the assumption that the message from up front should vary depending upon the audience, and that spiritual growth is a matter of progress or ladder-climbing, rather than a perpetual cycle of confession and absolution. This tendency is typically on display wherever one finds a distinction being drawn between "evangelism" (the message to non-believers) and "discipleship" (the message for believers). Some churches add a second level of stratification by emphasizing a difference between "baby Christians" and "mature Christians" – those feeding upon milk and those feeding upon meat, "the Timothys and the Pauls." AA consciously eschews the suggestion that one drunk is superior or inferior in sobriety to the next. This lack of stratification among the members of AA is a crucial contributing ingredient to its health and growth.

But primarily, AA's success lies in the dynamic of "grace" as it plays out in the world of Twelve Step groups. AA offers a something-for-nothing exchange. Brokenness is met with warmth and not judgment, and that single emphasis shapes the program from top to bottom. It offers free, time-tested help to all who care to seek it. There are no requirements, dues, fees, or even expectations of the newcomer who walks into their first AA meeting. The message itself is the only commodity. If it appeals to you, then you can have it. In fact, people will bend over backwards to help you to find it, expecting nothing in return and considering the opportunity they've been given to help to be a personal privilege for them. Episcopal Bishop Edward Salmon is fond of saying: "If that's what you want, then that's what you should have." Such is the sentiment in AA: have as much or as little as you like, but know that your engagement with AA is an issue between you and God, not you and the fellow members of your congregation.

Because of this approach, the openly acknowledged fact in AA that each member is far from holy is always being underscored. AAs have mostly lived tragic lives. They have smoked too many cigarettes, wrecked too many cars, done too many deceitful things ever to feel justified in their own skin. The result is that people in "the program" will fight to keep themselves and others from being overly self-righteous, judgmental, rigid or serious. When a newcomer walks into a room, that person is not expected to be anything other than a mess. Failure is the price of admission. One does far worse in AA to deny one's weakness than to acknowledge it. Unlike in most arenas of life, in AA, the downside of life is played up. The results speak for themselves. A classic line from the *12 & 12* posits: "Pain [is] the touchstone of *all* spiritual progress" (93-94).

By way of contrast, it is not uncommon for churches to create an environment where people cannot really be open and honest about their (continued) struggles. They typically give off the white-washed impression of success where the leading of "good" moral lives are concerned, in spite of the fact that usually the opposite is in fact the case. Ask any minister about the "behind-the-scenes" life of his/her congregation and you will quickly hear this verified. Divorce, for example, runs rampant in the Christian community, just like it does outside of the church. The same goes for mental illness, substance abuse, domestic discord, tragic accidents, etc… On a related note, in Martin Luther's day, many of his own parishioners complained, "Why are you preaching the same thing still after all these years?" His response: "Because you still haven't understood it."

Such facts might shock a Christian who has been led to believe otherwise, but AA understands these realities, finding in each instance of besetting weakness an avenue for trusting in God more. The person in AA who denies the fact of sin in the sober life is nothing more than a liar. To quote 1 John 1: "If we claim to be without sin, we deceive ourselves." Yet it is possible to come into church on the grounds of an entirely different persona (e.g., "I'm an experienced, life-long Christian, a leader in the last church where I was a member. When would you like for me to start teaching Sunday School?"). In AA membership, there is only the option of sinner: "My name is John, and I'm an alcoholic."

It is also worth bearing in mind that some AAs tend to think the category of sinner applies only to alcoholics or other serious addicts. There is often talk in meetings about two kinds of humans: "alcoholics" and (normal) "earth people." The two conceivably cannot make heads or tails of each other. Alcoholics understand alcoholics, and earth people understand earth people. The alcoholic may find that she has a lot in common with a drug addict or even a gambling addict, but she has nothing in common with the those people out there who don't struggle with the problem of personal powerlessness and the compulsive behavioral meltdowns that accompany it. This view is naïve.

Traditional Christian theology, in contrast, understands the universalities that unite and define *all* people. The Church teaches that addiction displays, in fact, the true nature of what it means to be a human being living in a fallen world. The bridge between the alcoholic and the non-alcoholic is called sin, and faith affirms that the alcoholic has no greater need for God's grace than the "earth person" does, even if the circumstances in one case appear to be more dire. Both people will die, and both people need love. The same is true for both men and women, people of different races and ages and cultures – it's universal. Is the cancer patient who feels "fine" really any less sick than the depressed person who cannot get out of bed? We are all equal in sin and personal powerlessness, and although some manifestations may be more destructive than others, to obsess over one particular expression of sin is to misinterpret the data. For this reason, church leaders would do well to recall Christianity's notion of the bound will. The fruit of this idea is a compassion borne out of a stark honesty about the human condition.

The Message, Not the Messenger

"Then the Lord opened the donkey's mouth, and it said to Balaam..."
-Numbers 22:28

"And we have ceased fighting anything or anyone"
-Big Book (85)

Where the Bible talks about God speaking through "earthen vessels", in AA the earthen vessels appear to be especially cracked and ill-suited for the job of teaching. It is in part from the obvious modesty of the members that God seems to be able to speak so loudly through the group. There is a basic idea in AA that each member of the group is no better than any other. Because of this, no member of the group is completely right about anything. No member of AA can speak for AA. You can only speak for yourself.

This amounts to a sense that each member is but a heretic unless God chooses to speak through the mouth of such an individual (which He often does). In AA meetings, in other words, God speaks exclusively through the mouth of Balaam's ass. This benefits the listener in two ways.

First, *in AA there is no fear of heresy*. In fact, heretics get to speak their mind in every meeting. They are shown as much respect as are the wisest old-timers in the room. The voice of heresy is not viewed as a threat to the truth because true wisdom has its own unimpeachable stature.

Second, AA understands that it is possible to learn from bad teaching (about good teaching). It can strengthen one's beliefs far more than avoiding to engage with alternative positions. In church history terms, this means that Pelagius gets to preach in every meeting, and sometimes Augustine only gets a few brief minutes to rebut. But that is fine. Again, good old-fashioned Twelve-Step sobriety is not threatened by other less worthy contenders, and so there is no safe-guarding against their presence in the rooms of AA. This means that there is little fighting in AA over "theology." Or at the least, such fighting is considered to be highly counterproductive. In AA, all fighting is considered to be unhelpful.

That God chooses to speak profoundly about Himself through the mouths of ragamuffins and ne'er-do-wells strikes this writer as being somehow deeply good. The Bible offers great precedent for this kind of thing. That God would choose to start so influential a world religion from a backwater like Nazareth and with only the help of some country bumpkin, no-diploma fishermen boggles the mind. Crazy people in AA meetings often say smart things. Balaam's ass should be AA's mascot.

This approach works so well, in part, because AA does not have any official power structure or hierarchy. There is every drunk, and then there is God. In this respect, leaders in AA function much more like deacons than priests or bishops. Hypothetically, the moment that one individual wields more power than another, this model would most likely break down, with the message itself becoming the primary victim of dilution.[104] In effect, fighting would become necessary in order to hold onto the torch of classic AA sobriety. But that would also simultaneously contradict the message itself: "And we have ceased fighting anything or anyone" (85).

So how then do AAs resolve disputes about the program? *Validity in AA is demonstrated through competition rather than battle.* The cream rises to the top; the good tree bears good fruit. Sound doctrine eclipses false doctrine primarily by outshining it. In the Church, on the other hand, leaders spend an inordinate amount of time and energy actively trying to sanitize and protect doctrine from all error. The inevitable conflicts often lead to an embarrassing amount of fracture and dissolution. In one case in the upstate of South Carolina, I remember hearing of a church that split over the issue of home-schooling, and whether or not all kids should receive such an education.

In contrast, AAs find rest in the knowledge that the extreme fallen-ness of the alcoholic temperament, even in sobriety, quickly reveals the limitations of a heretical approach to sobriety by displaying its catastrophic implications.

---

[104] Along these lines, Bill Wilson wrote in a letter to Sam Shoemaker:

"St. Louis [the conference where Bill stepped down from his role as AA's official leader] was a major step toward my own withdrawal, but I understand that the father symbol will always be hitched to me. Therefore, the problem is not how to get rid of parenthood; it is how to discharge mature parenthood properly.

A dictatorship always refuses to do this, and so do the hierarchical churches. They sincerely feel that their several families can never be enough educated (or spiritualized) to properly guide their own destinies. Therefore, people who have to live within the structure of dictatorships and hierarchies must lose, to a greater or lesser degree, the opportunity of really growing up. I think AA can avoid this temptation to concentrate its power, and I truly believe that it is going to be intelligent enough and spiritualized enough to rely on [God as he expresses Himself in] our group conscience."

Don't Tell Me What To Do! The Relationship Between Spirituality and Morality

This need-based model of spirituality brings with it a distinct and unavoidable implication for community life: people in AA are quick to draw attention to personal failings, but they place little emphasis upon morality. "We do not wish to be the arbiters of anyone's conduct" (69). This means that AA provides a community environment that is simultaneously deeply concerned with God's active work in the life of people, and deeply unconcerned with telling people what to do or what they should do. The response to almost all moral conundrums and life decisions is: "Have you prayed about it?" The notion that God alone knows what needs to be done, and that, without Him, all effort is of little merit, is paramount in AA.

In effect, AA's primary orientation is vertical (man to God) rather than horizontal (man to man). Morality comes from God, not people, and dictating what people should do is understood in AA as indicative of a lack of faith in God's ability to act. A critical, prescriptive attitude actually quenches spiritual inspiration. Thus, the only command issued in AA operates along the line of: "Find God or else..." When God is found, hindrances are naturally faced and dealt with. The results tend to be inspiring.

I remember the story one long-time member of AA told of his work as a mentor to a newcomer to sobriety, known in the program as the sponsor-sponsee relationship:

> "My faith was really put to the test with this one kid I sponsored. He started dating a girl who was brand new in the program when he was only six months sober. It's the kind of thing that tends to be a recipe for disaster.
>
> They had a brief 'honeymoon' period and ended up moving in together. It was not long after that that

the girl started drinking again. She spiraled quickly into a deep mire of depression and alcoholism, and my sponsee became her sole care-giver, arguably her 'enabler'. Everyone knew the situation was terrible, that his sobriety hung in the balance, and that he was getting in the way of her hitting bottom, thereby prolonging her agony. We all used to get together after meetings and talk about their terrible situation and how he needed to get out of there pronto.

But my job as his sponsor was not to tell him what to do; it was to point him to God and encourage him to seek God's guidance in all things...So we would get together each week for coffee and I'd ask how things were going. The story was always bad, and it took huge amounts of self-restraint for me to not tell him to just get the hell out of there. But I would always ask the following question, as was/is my duty as a sponsor: 'Are you praying about it?'

To my disappointment, his answer was always 'yes.' One day, after months of this awfulness, I reached the end of my fuse and decided to try to steer him a bit; I asked him: 'Which decision would require more faith from you: to stay with her, or to leave her?' I couldn't believe his answer: 'Definitely to stay with her.' After that I just told him to 'keep praying.'

So get this. One day he showed up for coffee with news. She went to an AA meeting by herself. Next thing you know, the girl has a sponsor, she's going to tons of AA meetings, she's working the steps, logging in a string of days of continuous sobriety...Nine months go by and the girl is still sober, super-involved, completely unlike her first round in the program. Soon, the couple gets engaged. Two years later, they're married, both sober and happy, and they own and run a bar together in Brooklyn. And she always cites how grateful she is that he weathered that terrible time with her without leaving.

As it turns out, none of us knew better than God."

This rather hands-off approach to counseling is born not only out of an inability to give good advice, but also out of a low estimation of a person's capacity for receiving "good advice". The problem lies both in the desire to advise, and in the defensiveness and rebellion that is often sparked/instigated by criticism.

AA's 9th Tradition attempts to translate this principle to the governance of the larger body, and the formulation is striking: "AA, as such, ought never be organized." This approach was inherited directly from the Oxford group, whose motto with regard to all moral questioning was: "Do whatever God lets you!" This posture is markedly absent from so many churches.

Consider the following passages where Bill Wilson describes the thinking behind the 9th Tradition:

> "Did anyone ever hear of a nation, a church, a political party, even a benevolent association that had no membership rules? Did anyone ever hear of a society which couldn't somehow discipline its members and enforce obedience to necessary rules and regulations? ...Power to direct or govern is the essence of organization everywhere.
>
> Yet AA is an exception. It does not conform to this pattern. Neither its General Service Conference, its Foundation Board, nor the humblest group committee can issue a single directive to an AA member and make it stick, let alone mete out any punishment. We've tried it lots of times, but utter failure is always the result.

> At this juncture, we can hear a churchman exclaim, "They are making disobedience a virtue!" He is joined by the psychiatrist who says, "Defiant brats! They won't grow up and conform to social usage!" The man in the street says, "I don't understand it. They must be nuts!" But all these observers have overlooked something unique in AA. Unless each AA member follows to the best of his ability our suggested Twelve Steps to recovery, he almost certainly signs his own death warrant. His drunkenness and dissolution are not penalties inflicted by people in authority; they result from his personal disobedience to spiritual principles.
>
> ...So we of AA do obey spiritual principles, first because we must, and ultimately because we love the kind of life such obedience brings. *Great suffering and great love are AA's disciplinarian; we need no others."* (*12 & 12*, 172-174)

It is important not to disregard the way in which a low anthropology motivates a proportionally high view of God's work.[105] By admitting our weakness in the face of God's total sovereignty over our salvation *and* sanctification, both recognition of God's rescuing work and genuine human-to-human compassion spring forth.

Most AA meetings close with the group standing in a circle, holding hands. Then the following is said by the person who volunteered to lead the meeting: "Would those who care to please

---

[105] Theologically speaking, it seems to be the case that AA has managed to avoid falling into the world of "antinomianism", which is the idea that, when a person is given freedom from the law, they will naturally seek to abuse such leniency by acting immorally and without any qualms about it. Using this passage from the 9th Tradition, we see that, where the dire verdict hoisted over the head of every person who professes alcoholism is present, responsibility and uprightness usually result. One can extrapolate that where the law precedes the reception of the Gospel, antinomianism becomes a non-issue.

join me in saying the Lord's Prayer: *Who keeps us sober? ...Our Father who art in heaven..."*

Christian Concerns About AA: The Source, The Name, and the AA Straw Man

Despite the apparent similarities between traditional Christian doctrine and the flourishing, church-like communal life on display in AA, one might ask whether or not the source of sobriety and sanctification in AA is the same as the source of 'spiritual fruit' described in the Bible? It is a good question. Personally, I believe that the redemptive love of God comes from Jesus into the world in the presence of the Holy Spirit. Where there is redemption to be found, then there too is Christ. Where there is healing, there is the presence of the Great Physician. The Holy Spirit must be present for redemptive work to occur in the rooms of AA. After all, the Spirit is not some parlor trick for humans to manipulate simply by saying a magic word. Jesus said: "The wind blows wherever it pleases. You hear its sound, but you cannot tell where it comes from or where it is going. So it is with everyone born of the Spirit" (John 3:8).

Furthermore, it is very difficult to calculate where there is progress and improvement in a person's life, especially one's own. AA is quick to affirm that God often uses the shortcomings of a person more significantly than their supposed strengths. In other words, being overly concerned with locating and quantifying the work of God (a.k.a. the instinct to pinpoint and/or measure the source of redemptive power) can be counterproductive and even dangerous. The very question of self-improvement smacks of self-righteousness, or at least the inclination toward it.

As we mentioned earlier, in AA there is only talk of God as the rescuer of troubled people. Some people worry that the Christian material contained in AA is not phrased in explicitly Christian terminology. For example, the word "Jesus" is rarely used. To our way of thinking, the fact that God in AA is always understood to operate in a soteriological way is actually impressive, as well as fundamentally Christian.

We might even take this one step further and say that any person who calls on the God who saves is a Christian, whether they know it or not. This does not mean that everyone in AA is a Christian, but it does imply that there are many people in AA who do not attend church but are nonetheless Christians.

There is also the more general distaste that some in the Christian community seem to have for AA. This is especially true in the circles of thought most familiar with Reformation theology. Even the slightest mention of AA often provokes an intensely negative, knee-jerk reaction from otherwise seemingly charitable theologians. Such responses usually betray a fear of the unknown, and a "straw man" understanding of a world of thought with which they are not very familiar. There is a concern that to affirm that there is real truth and spiritual insight in AA would somehow be to affirm a syncretistic approach to Christianity. In this book, we have tried to explain why such criticisms are unfounded and lacking in insight. Of course, the two trains of thought can be at odds with each other, but they are not necessarily so.

We have tried to show where such concerns do and don't have a bearing on the factual material as it stands. Obviously, we think AA and Christianity have more rather than less in common with each other, and not the other way around.

Pastoral Care for the Addicted

For the unbelieving husband has been sanctified through his believing wife, and the unbelieving wife has been sanctified through her believing husband. Otherwise your children would be unclean, but as it is, they are holy.
-1 Corinthians 7:14

Perhaps it comes as no surprise that the best way to help those who are struggling with active addiction is to send them to AA, or the appropriate Twelve Step group. Until they deal with their addiction, the church can do very little for an alcoholic in his/her cups.

This assertion raises some legitimate concerns for Christians. Would we really recommend AA over and above church involvement? Some Christians find this idea troubling.

Directing an alcoholic to a church service instead of an AA group is like asking novices to deal with a situation that requires experts – when there are millions of experts close by. The alcoholic needs to be directed to the place where they will hear about the God who saves drunks.

Along the same lines, many parents who express happiness about the fact that their young adult child has found sobriety in a Twelve Step group lament the child's continued distaste for the church life that means so much to them. In such situations, the long view is to be encouraged. Space, encouragement and love are to be given to the child, not religious pressure. At all costs, affirm their Twelve Step work and AA involvement. In many cases, it is only a matter of time before the sober individual's Christian faith becomes ignited. Parents need to hear: "You just watch, pray and wait. Your faith will work like a tractor beam." Usually, after the excruciating years of parenting a child struggling with substance abuse and addiction, sobriety in any form is enough to convince an exhausted parent that God is in fact taking care of their child. The return to church involvement is simply the cherry on the top of the sundae.

What Can the Church Offer AA?

"Not all of us join religious bodies, but most of us favor such memberships... Be quick to see where religious people are right"
-*Big Book (28, 87).*

Despite the lessons that AA's understanding of human nature and God's work can teach the Church, Step 11 makes it clear that the recovering alcoholic needs the Church, too. Most importantly, the Church has the story. The old, old story of 'Jesus and his glory'. The God of salvation is a revelation, grounded in a very specific set of historical truths that undergird and underline the spiritual realities that the addict has experienced. God is more than a subjective truth – He is an objective reality.

Of course, as we have noted throughout, the Church does not always do the story justice. Often it puts the cart before the horse. Sometimes it even gives the wrong story, stating that Christianity is about morality rather than forgiveness of immoral people, about good people getting better, not bad people coping with their failure to be good. But when the Church gives the right story, the story of the death and resurrection of Jesus Christ, "the friend of sinners" – a story which deeply coheres with the insights of AA – nothing could be more powerful or profound or positive. The spiritual picture painted in Twelve Step recovery comes into amazing focus, and vice versa. The TV show changes from black-and-white to Blu-Ray high-definition color.

Alcoholics Anonymous does a brilliant job of bringing the reality of human failings together with the saving grace of a God who is present in the day-to-day aspects of human life. The front half of the Twelve Steps underscores the importance of holding onto the Christian doctrine of original sin. But the second half of the Twelve Steps, which seek to enable the individual to deepen their spirituality benefits hugely from the road that has been trod by countless Christians before them. Thus, it makes sense that, as a study of this sort progresses through the Twelve Steps, more and more theological material would come to define the landscape of the life described.

The main principle at work in the Twelve Steps is that God shows up to meet the defeated and the weak, the lowly and the paralyzed. It is a principle that Jesus enacted and taught repeatedly throughout his ministry. He said, "It is not the healthy who need a doctor, but the sick. I have not come to call the righteous but sinners" (Mark 2:17). To the extent that people acknowledge their failings, they find and appreciate Him. And because there is so much honest acknowledgement of that reality in the world of AA and addiction, one very often finds more redemption, more actual healing and more transformation than in the Church – in spite of the fact that these are the same people who know themselves still to be addicts.

In closing, the Church would benefit tremendously from the presence of more Twelve Steppers in its pews. No one can help Christians reconnect with the heart of their own message better than sober alcoholics. This word of "love for the loveless shown", distilled so profoundly in AA, is not only what Christians need to reclaim for themselves; it is also what the wounded world at large so desperately craves. It works where other approaches fail. It heals where other approaches hurt. It brings hope where there is none to be had because it is Hope itself.

Epilogue: "But the Lord…"

Whitney Houston and the Difference Between Sobriety and Faith

"On hearing this, Jesus said to them, 'It is not the healthy who need a doctor, but the sick. I have not come to call the righteous, but sinners.'
-*Mark 2:17*

"However, to the one who does not work but trusts God who justifies the ungodly, their faith is credited as righteousness."
-*Romans 4:5*

A wise woman in AA once remarked, "I ain't got to feel God, in order to know God. I'm sober, ain't I?!" Her point was that spirituality does not depend upon a particular emotional state in order to be credible and real. This woman's sentiment reflects spiritual maturity, in that she acknowledges the reality of suffering in sobriety without abandoning a belief in God. In AA, the sober alcoholic can find encouragement in the mere fact of sobriety, even if nothing else in her life seems to be improving. Sobriety is understood to be the obvious evidence of God's presence in the alcoholic's life.

But Christian thinking pushes the issue even further by asking whether or not God can be present even in the life of the alcoholic who cannot stay sober. When someone falls off the wagon, is it due to a lack of faith? Perhaps this relapse is a sign that he was never a part of the AA "elect" in the first place. In response to this concern, the Gospel message suggests most amazingly that God may be even closer to the alcoholic who cannot remain sober than He is to the one who has found sobriety. [106] Luther famously remarked that God is closest to the one who appears to be furthest from Him.[107] To put it in stark theological terms, the primary issue in Christianity is faith itself – not the elusive, and sometimes imperceptible, fruit born of faith.

Those who ultimately value the justification of the sinner by faith in Christ to be the core of Christianity can indeed affirm that true spirituality is a matter of faith and not works. In most cases, where faith (of the AA variety that we have been at pains to describe) is present in the heart of the alcoholic, we will not need to draw a biblical distinction of this type. Usually, sobriety is a natural counterpart to newfound faith. Good trees typically bear good fruit. On occasion, however, it may be the case that faith, in and of itself, is the only *perceptible* fruit.

A prime example of this came to the fore during the writing of this book in the death of singer Whitney Houston. A notorious

---

[106] I was struck by the implications of this train of thought in an AA meeting where I heard a man report that his brother had died of alcoholism after years of failed attempts at sobriety. His comment: "In the case of my brother, the only hope for him was death itself. My family and I take comfort in knowing that he is close to God now."

[107] Paraphrased from Martin Luther, "Sermon on Matthew 20:1-16", in vol. 2 of *Sermons of Martin Luther: the Seven Volumes* (Grand Rapids, MI: Baker Books, 2000), 109.

drug addict whose history of substance abuse culminated in her death by an overdose in a bathtub, Whitney made the front page of papers across the world. And so did her funeral, where the playwright and filmmaker Tyler Perry contributed a profound message. He made clear the good news of the Gospel: that forgiveness and redemption stand firm most poignantly in the places where sin appears to be dominant. He used her life to illustrate how the love of God comes to us "in spite of" our sin.

We quote from the transcript of his speech. He began by describing a conversation he had with Whitney four years earlier in a restaurant in Atlanta:

> "... she was telling me about her life. She would talk about some things that she had went through. Some things that had made her sad, some things that were tough. As [she spoke], I would see this heaviness come upon her... But before I could get words out to encourage her, she would say "but the Lord..." And the conversation went on, and we would talk a little bit more. She would go back into sadness and just when I'm about to step in, she would say "but my Lord and my Savior, Jesus Christ and his amazing grace..." It was at that moment that I knew that I would do all I can to stand with her...
>
> When I think about her, there's a scripture that keeps burning in my heart. I keep thinking about the Apostle Paul in Romans when he is talking about, 'I am persuaded that nothing shall separate me from the love of God.' (Rom 8:39) [Paul] was describing her life so perfectly... No matter how far she went in the stratosphere, no matter how much struggle, no matter what she had to go through, it still wasn't enough to separate her from the love of God. So what I know

about Whitney is that she loved the Lord. And if there was a grace that carried her all the way through, it was the same grace that carried her home.

And I want to close with something else the Apostle Paul said: 'What then say you to these things, that if God be for you, who can be against you?' (Rom 8:31) So say whatever you want; God was for her, and she is resting, singing with the angels."

His words absolutely drip with the promise of faith!

While I don't know about Whitney Houston personally, I do know about what the Christian faith offers to Whitney-Houston "types"…and it is good news: God loves Whitney-Houston types as much as He loves anyone. This is the bittersweet side of the Gospel message, which people despise unless, of course, they know themselves to be in the same group as the Whitney Houstons of the world. People hated this about Jesus' message two thousand years ago. "He sups with sinners and tax-collectors", they complained. We might be inclined to think that this much grace is *too* much. It "passeth all understanding" (Ph 4:7, KJV). But such is the promise of faith, regardless of anything.

St. Anthony's is a home for alcoholics in Minnesota where these ideas are pushed to their furthest implications. Unlike most rehabilitative centers for alcoholism, where drinking is typically viewed as grounds for dismissal, the residents of St. Anthony's are allowed to drink alcohol in their rooms without hindrance. It is a "wet house", the only one of its kind that we are aware of. A reporter from *This American Life* describes the scene:

> "Walking down the hallway I could hear muffled TVs playing in their rooms, and I got the sense that people

are slowly killing themselves behind closed doors. During that year when ten guys went into treatment, three of the residents died."

In his book *This American Gospel,* writer Ethan Richardson offers the following by way of explanation: "St. Anthony's is predicated upon unconditional love…They will celebrate and encourage a resident's recovery, but one's invitation is not revoked if recovery does not happen"[108] (79). In other words, St. Anthony's is motivated by an understanding of Christian love and hope that runs deeper than the individual's ability to respond to it. When asked whether it is hard to accept the self-defeating behavior on display, staff member Deacon Jim says:

> "Yeah, it is hard. It is hard. But we care for them where they are. If they're ready to move, [or] if they're not ready to move. That's really not our call here. Our call is to love them."

In the extreme world of alcoholism, that most tragic group – those who die drunk – deserves consideration. In spite of death's seeming finality, the Christian understanding of life offers a hope that the world cannot see. It views addiction, even in death, through the lens of grace.

We close with another sermon excerpt, this time taken from the rector of Christ Episcopal Church, Charlottesville, Paul Walker. He tells of his brother-in-law:

> "Robbie was my wife Christie's older brother. Robbie was 6 foot 4 inches, dark and handsome – he had dark auburn hair and a full beard. He had magnetic looks. An

---

[108] Ethan Richardson, *This American Gospel* (Charlottesville, VA: Mockingbird, 2012), 79.

artist once asked him to pose as Jesus! He had a carefree personality; everybody loved Robbie; he was always where the excitement was.

In our living room, we have a picture of Robbie on the docks of Cape Hatteras. He has just returned from a deep-sea fishing trip and is holding up a 7 foot blue marlin. He looks like a cross between Jesus and Ernest Hemingway, his muscles taut with the fish's prodigious weight. Clearly, this is one of Robbie's better days.

Robbie's better days did not last. As he grew older he struggled with alcoholism. At one point Robbie confessed to me, "Paul, this thing is a monster. It's just too big for me." As Robbie suffered, we suffered with him.

What Robbie called his darkest night happened during a stint in rehab. He was alone in a detox room, facing his demons by himself. It was three in the morning and he was terrified. Robbie was never a church-goer —but in that dark night Robbie experienced light and hope and love. Afterward he said, "This sounds really weird, but in that awful night I felt Jesus with me. He came to me. I knew everything was going to be okay."

Robbie died about a year later. The monster was finally too big for him. He died alone, but he was not by himself. Christie has a vivid image of Jesus cradling Robbie as he died. I imagine Jesus' face close to Robbie's, saying, 'Don't be afraid. In my Father's house there are many rooms. This is no idle tale. If it were not so, would I have told you that I go to prepare a place for you?'

Easter means that we do not look for Robbie among the dead but among the living. Easter means that

Robbie is alive with Jesus, fit and strong and smiling on the everlasting docks, free of his and every other monster. Easter means that for Robbie, for us, for you, and for the world that Jesus came not to condemn but to save, everything is going to be okay. The Better Day will prevail. Amen."

Grace is the hope that seeks us out when we are at our worst. It looks forward to the long, hard road ahead. Grace is not worried, even if everything falls apart and everything goes wrong. It is the love of God that does not let go. It brings good out of bad, and it sees hope where there is none. Grace always gives another chance. Grace waits. It stands when you have fallen; it leaves the door open. Grace stays awake for you when you can't keep your eyes open for another minute, even though you know you should.

Grace works like Mrs. Luella Bates Washington Jones, who talks with a boy she caught stealing her purse:[109]

> "If I turn you loose, will you run?" asked the woman.
>
> "Yes'm," said the boy.
>
> "Then I won't turn you loose," said the woman. She did not release him. [She takes him to her home, and tells him to wash his face]
>
> "You gonna take me to jail?" asked the boy, bending over the sink.
>
> "Not with that face, I wouldn't take you nowhere," said the woman. "Here I am trying to get home to cook me a bite to eat and you snatch my pocketbook! Maybe you ain't been to your supper either, late as it be. Have you?"

---

[109] Excerpt from Langston Hughes, "Thank You, Ma'am", New York, NY: SRA/McGraw-Hill, 1997.

"There's nobody home at my house," said the boy.

"Then we'll eat," said the woman.

[After supper she brings out dessert.] Then she cut him a half of her ten-cent cake.

"Eat some more, son," she said.

Grace is the overarching, never-say-never, covenantal, all-encompassing, law-subsuming, utterly distinct, absolutely committed, won't-take-no-for-an-answer, able to jump over a building in a single bound, non-neurotic, calming, spice-of-life, surprising, unexpected, unwavering, indissoluble voice of God:

"A bruised reed I will not break; a smoldering wick I will not snuff out."
-Isaiah 42:3

"If we are faithless, He will remain faithful."
-2 Tim 2:13

Appendix I: Mortimers and Lulus

Is the Person Who Got Sober in High School Really an Alcoholic?

"Many people, nonalcoholics, report that as a result of the practice of A.A.'s Twelve Steps they have been able to meet other difficulties in life. They think that Twelve Steps can mean more than sobriety for problem drinkers. They see in them a way to happy and effective living for many, alcoholic or not."
-12 & 12 (16)

A friend from early sobriety, who joined AA while he was in high school, wrote to me expressing doubts about whether or not he was actually an alcoholic. It's not an altogether uncommon situation. There are so many rehabs and therapeutic schools for troubled teenagers. Many of these institutions funnel their students into AA at a young age, even though some of them may have had little actual experience with drinking. We offered the following response. Maybe it will be helpful to you or someone you know:

Hi Travis,

Thanks so much for writing...

You've been sober a long time and in AA for almost two decades. It's obviously been an important experience and helped to shape you. From reading your email, I get the impression that the main question you have is whether or not you are actually an alcoholic.

That's an important question to ask — one that I asked myself at a similar age — and it's a particularly hard question for people who get sober as young as we did to ask. So we grow into adults in sobriety, and we ask ourselves, "Did I even garner enough experience with alcohol to even know if I can't control it? Was I just a party-kid? etc..."

I have no doubt that the Twelve Steps would have a positive and relevant impact on any person's life, whether they're alcoholic or not. I've actually led classes at my church (I called it "spiritual makeover"), taking normal people through the Twelve Steps. Every one of them benefited. Things like looking at "our part" in a resentment, being of service to others, making amends, prayer, etc. are all absolutely life-altering skills to learn for any person. They make sense in the face of life, more than most other therapeutic and spiritual approaches I have found. AA's Twelve Steps and the experience of attending meetings offer a profound method for learning to deal with life responsibly and spiritually. Who wouldn't benefit from the Twelve Steps, right? So I would say that the fact that you got a lot out of AA, and that it helped you to put the dots together with your life, doesn't really answer the question of whether or not you need to be an active member.

That question really has to do with whether or not you can control drinking alcohol. You're obviously not looking at it from the standpoint of wanting to rage and party and stain (i.e., go on a bender). I wonder if you can or cannot drink without it damaging all the other areas of your life. I also assume you're not wanting to see if you can "smoke a little pot" or whatever. I would advise you to steer clear of other drugs, which is a no-brainer, especially since they're illegal in most places. So I'm just talking about drinking, really. The distinction between heavy partying and alcoholism is not one that I could have made when I was in high school, as they were both part of the same lifestyle to me. But then we grow up, and it turns out that the drinking of wine and cocktails and beer is a different thing entirely than it was in high school or college.

So can Travis X drink a glass or two of wine at a dinner party, or order a cocktail when he's out at a bar with friends or on a date with his wife? I don't know. Do you think he could? I've seen AAs who have gotten sober young ask themselves that exact question on multiple occasions.

The first way that I think AA would help a person to answer that question is to look back at their past experience with drinking. Did you drink enough in high school to figure out whether or not there's an actual pattern of lacking control? That's the key issue that determines whether or not you're an alcoholic in the eyes of AA, right?

If you think the answer is yes, then probably you shouldn't start drinking, as that pattern is probably still there. If it's "no" or "maybe", then you might try drinking responsibly, because I don't think "maybe" is a good enough answer to justify continued involvement in AA in your case. Maybe set some guidelines for yourself about it, and see if you can adhere to them. You can keep me posted on how that goes if you like. I would talk that one over with your wife beforehand, just so that she too is abreast of watching to see if you can control your drinking.

Here's what I've seen: I had a sponsor named Mortimer who got sober at 17. He was an amazing member of AA and worked as a graphic designer for a big company. Do you know the saying, "There's a slip under every skirt?" Well he started drinking again when he turned 26 after a break-up and was literally homeless and deeply drug-addicted, following Phish on tour and couch-surfing within two months of picking up that first drink. He was drunk at work the second week after he started drinking again and lost his job almost immediately thereafter. The guy was an alcoholic of the first degree. He's still out there and has yet to rediscover sobriety, though he desperately needs to. He's in bad shape, and he will not be able to sort things out with his family and life until he sobers up. That's my opinion, but there are obvious reasons why I feel that way.

Then there's my good friend Lulu, who got sober a few years after finishing college. She got all into AA, got a sponsor, worked the steps, and was four months sober when we first reconnected. She stayed sober for five years, but she moved to a new city during her third year of sobriety. She only went to a few meetings after the move and soon started asking all the same questions you're asking. "Was I actually an alcoholic?" She benefited hugely from the steps and from adopting the AA approach to life, but she wondered if the Twelve Steps had worked with her vulnerability more than with an actual alcohol problem. And bear in mind that Lulu actually did a fair amount of drinking and partying, both in college and afterwards.

So finally, after five years sober and two years without meetings, she decided, after discussing it with some friends from AA, to order a glass of wine at a dinner with her husband. She's been drinking again socially and a having a glass or two of wine at home on occasion for more than two years, and it's turned out not to be a problem. She got really black-out drunk once, when an old friend from high school showed up and got her to take a bunch of shots – which is not her style – but nothing severe or troubling otherwise. She still functions as a responsible human being and values the Twelve Steps, which she still makes use of. She doesn't need to be sober in order to be of service to other people, to hold down a job, etc for the Twelve Steps to work for her.

That's the difference between an alcoholic and a non-alcoholic. The truth is that there are both Mortimers and Lulus in AA. The Mortimers can't drink. The Lulus can.

Are you a Mortimer or a Lulu? I think you might be a Lulu, no offense. ;) What do you think? Is this helpful? Keep me posted and let me know what you decide. I would love to track with you on it...

Cheers, bioluminescently yours, JZ

P.S. What I've said lines up with the Big Book, I think: *"If anyone who is showing inability to control his drinking can do the right-about-face and drink like a gentleman, our hats are off to him…you can quickly diagnose yourself. Step over to the nearest barroom and try some controlled drinking. Try to drink and stop abruptly. Try it more than once. It will not take long for you to decide, if you are honest with yourself…" (31-32).*

Appendix II: Mingling with Alcohol in Sobriety

"In our belief any scheme of combating alcoholism which proposes to shield the sick man from temptation is doomed to failure."
-*Big Book (101)*

Nothing outside a person can defile them by going into them. Rather, it is what comes out of a person that defiles them."
-*Mark 7:15*

So what are we to do about the presence of alcohol in the midst of a sober life? Very little, if anything! The fact that lots of people in the world drink while many alcoholics are in the midst of getting sober is of little concern. Here again, we find that AA's insight is somewhat counter-intuitive. Alcoholism is understood in AA to be an inner problem, and not an outer one: "Any scheme of combating alcoholism which proposes to shield the sick man from temptation is doomed to failure" (101).

To the outsider looking in, the assumption typically is that sobriety is first and foremost about learning how to effectively avoid alcohol. Taking such an approach overestimates the power of the alcoholic's will power with respect to alcohol and, in effect, misunderstands the problem and solution that thousands of people have found in AA.

Instead, sobriety is about experiencing a spiritual change that comes from God's grace through the working of the Twelve Steps. In discussing Step 10, the Big Book describes the sobriety of a "spiritually fit" alcoholic in the following terms:

> "And we have ceased fighting anything or anyone – even alcohol. For by this time sanity will have returned. We will seldom be interested in liquor. If tempted, we recoil from it as from a hot flame. We react sanely and normally, and we will find that this has happened automatically. We will see that our new attitude toward liquor has been given us without any thought or effort on our part. It just comes! That is the miracle of it. We are not fighting it, neither are we avoiding temptations. We feel as though we had been placed in a position of neutrality – safe and protected. We have not even sworn off. Instead, the problem has been removed. It does not exist for us. We are neither cocky nor are we afraid. That is our experience. That is how we react so long as we keep in fit spiritual condition." (85)

It is not uncommon for the significant other of a newly sober person to assume that they to need to adopt a life of sobriety. This may or may not be helpful, but people should certainly not assume it to be necessary. When the time is right, alcoholics can get sober regardless of any particular set of circumstances (98). Eventually, any form of healthy sobriety will realistically require the ability to be around alcohol without making a big deal about it. In many cases, the appropriate imbibing of others will actually strengthen the sobriety of the sober individual.

This happens for three reasons. First, it helps the sober alcoholic to see that, indeed, they have been granted reprieve from their besetting weakness. They are no longer the person they used to be. Such an experience is incredibly encouraging, and for the sober alcoholic who is actively involved in recovery, it will in no way lead to some kind of false assumption that they are cured for life.

Second, seeing the normal, convivial drinking of a non-alcoholic drives home the ongoing reality of the alcoholic's need for sobriety. I remember seeing my mother drink half a glass of wine while working on her taxes. That is not alcoholism.

Third, when people avoid drinking for the sake of the sober alcoholic, they are actually hoisting the state of his prior destructive life style over his head like a kind of guillotine. The impact can be a bit like being held in "time out", or placed in a penalty box. It can be a subtle form of punishment, a kind of holding the past against a person in a way that is unnecessary and also un-insightful. In most cases, the sober alcoholic feels immense relief the moment other people take that first drink in his or her presence without making a big deal about it. You may find that one of the best ways to minister to your sober friends is to have a drink or two in front of them.

Perhaps you are familiar with the Baptist Church's strict no-drinking-of-alcohol policy for all of their missionaries. The basic idea behind this approach suggests that any kind of indiscretion will damage their ability to effectively witness to the truth of the

Gospel. For the most part, AA disagrees with this approach in spite of its advocacy of sobriety for problem drinkers.[110]

AA instead suggests that they can more effectively share sobriety with the world (and especially with those in need of it) by not shunning alcohol. Shunning is viewed to be both counter-productive and ineffective for dealing with real alcoholism. Consequently, AA implies that drinking around recovering alcoholics is probably more helpful to them than not doing so.

The writers of the Big Book dealt with this issue at some length. They wanted to help the world to better understand their approach to sobriety. Please take the time to read the original source material that has fueled our thinking about this issue:

> "Assuming we are spiritually fit, we can do all sorts of things alcoholics are not supposed to do. People have said we must not go where liquor is served; we must not have it in our homes; we must shun friends who drink; we must avoid moving pictures which show drinking scenes; we must not go into bars; our friends must hide their bottles if we go to their houses; we mustn't think or be reminded about alcohol at all. Our experience shows that this is not necessarily so.
>
> "We meet these conditions every day. An alcoholic who cannot meet them, still has an alcoholic mind; there is something the matter with his spiritual status. His only chance for sobriety would be some place like the Greenland Ice Cap, and even there an

---

[110] Of course, the newly sober individual will need to separate themselves from alcohol in the initial experience of recovery. In-patient rehabs are recommended for this reason primarily. In such places, alcoholics can begin the much need work of the recovery and the Twelve Steps. Until the habit of attending meetings has become grooved, and the working of Twelve Steps is under way, the sober alcoholic is simply in between drinks, and far from transformed in the way that AA respects.

Eskimo might turn up with a bottle of scotch and ruin everything! Ask any woman who has sent her husband to distant places on the theory that he would escape the alcohol problem.

"In our belief any scheme of combating alcoholism which proposes to shield the sick man from temptation is doomed to failure. If the alcoholic tries to shield himself he may succeed for a time, but he usually winds up with a bigger explosion than ever. We have tried these methods. These attempts to do the impossible have always failed.

"So our one rule is not to avoid a place where there is drinking, if we have a legitimate reason for being there. That includes bars, nightclubs, dances, receptions, weddings, even plain ordinary whoopee parties. To a person who has had experience with an alcoholic, this may seem like tempting Providence, but it isn't...Your job now is to be at the place where you may be of maximum helpfulness to others, so never hesitate to go anywhere if you can be helpful. You should not hesitate to visit the most sordid spot on earth on such an errand. Keep on the firing line of life with these motives and God will keep you unharmed...

"We are careful never to show intolerance or hatred of drinking as an institution. Experience shows that such an attitude is not helpful to anyone. Every new alcoholic looks for this spirit among us and is immensely relieved when he finds we are not witch burners. A spirit of intolerance might repel alcoholics whose lives could have been saved, had it not been for such stupidity." (101-103)

Appendix III: The Serenity Prayer

God, give us grace to accept with serenity
the things that cannot be changed,
Courage to change the things
which should be changed,
and the Wisdom to distinguish
the one from the other.

Living one day at a time,
Enjoying one moment at a time,
Accepting hardship as a pathway to peace,
Taking, as Jesus did,
This sinful world as it is,
Not as I would have it,
Trusting that You will make all things right,
If I surrender to Your will,
So that I may be reasonably happy in this life,
And supremely happy with You forever in the next.
Amen.

-Reinhold Niebuhr

Bibliography

Allison, C. FitzSimons. *Fear, Love, and Worship*. Vancouver, British Columbia: Regent College Publishing, 2003.

Allison, C. FitzSimons. *The Rise of Moralism: The Proclamation of the Gospel from Hooker to Baxter*. Regent College Publishing, 2003.

B., Dick. *New Light on Alcoholism: God, Sam Shoemaker, and A.A.* 2nd ed. Kihei, HI: Paradise Research Publications, 1998.

Bonhoeffer, Dietrich. *Life Together*. Translated by John W. Doberstein. San Francisco: Harper & Row, 1954.

Brewer, Todd and David Zahl, ed. *The Gospel According to Pixar*. Charlottesville, VA: Mockingbird, 2010.

Brown, Steve. *Three Free Sins: God's Not Mad at You*. Brentwood, TN: Howard Books, 2012.

C., Chuck. *A New Pair of Glasses*. 10th ed. Irvine, CA: Chamberlain, 2008.

Creating a Sober World, Inc. *Absolutely Sober: A History, Principles, and Practice of the Deconstruction of Self-Centeredness*. Printed by CreateSpace Independent Publishing Platform, 2012.

Eagleman, David. *Incognito: The Secret Lives of the Brain*. New York, NY: Pantheon, 2011.

Eliot, George. *Scenes of a Clerical Life*. New York, NY: Oxford UP, 1988.

Forde, Gerhard. "A Lutheran Response", in *Christian Spirituality: Five Views of Sanctification*. Edited by Donald L. Alexander. Westmont, IL: Intervarsity, 1988.

Forde, Gerhard. *A More Radical Gospel: Essays on Eschatology, Authority, Atonement, and Ecumenism*. Edited by Mark C. Mattes and Steven D. Paulson. Lutheran Quarterly Books. Grand Rapids: Eerdmans, 2004.

Forde, Gerhard. *On Being a Theologian of the Cross: Reflections on Luther's Heidelberg Disputation, 1518*. Grand Rapids, MI: Eerdmans, 1997.

Holl, Karl. *The Reconstruction of Morality*. Edited by James Luther Adams and Walter F. Bense. Minneapolis, MN: Augsburg Publishing House, 1979.

Hughes, Langston. "Thank You, Ma'am." New York, NY: SRA/McGraw-Hill, 1997.

Karr, Mary. *Lit: A Memoir*. New York, NY: Penguin, 2005.

Kierkegaard, Søren. *The Sickness unto Death*. Translated by Howard H. Hong and Edna V. Hong. Princeton, NJ: Princeton UP, 1980.

Martyn, Dorothy. *Beyond Deserving*. Grand Rapids, MI: Eerdmans, 2007.

Mattes, Mark C., *The Role of Justification in Contemporary Theology*. Cambridge, UK: Eerdmans, 2004.

McRaney, David. "Procrastination." *You Are Not So Smart: A Celebration of Self Delusion* (blog). http://youarenotsosmart.com/2010/10/27/procrastination/

Meltzer, Erica. "Police: Boulder Man Shoots Self While Sleepwalking." *Boulder Daily Camera*. http://www.dailycamera.com/news/ci_16440985 Boulder

Rohr, Richard. *Breathing Under Water: Spirituality and the Twelve Steps*. Cincinnati, OH: St. Anthony Messenger Press, 2011.

Rohr, Richard. *Everything Belongs: The Gift of Contemplative Prayer*. New York, NY: The Crossroad Publishing Company, 2003.

Rosenbladt, Rod. *Christ Alone*. Wheaton, IL: Crossway Books, 1999.

Russell, A. J. *For Sinners Only*. Hats Off Books, 2003.

Schmidt, Richard H. *Glorious Companions: Five Centuries of Anglican Spirituality*. Grand Rapids, MI: Eerdmans, 2002.

Tavris, Carol and Elliot Aronson. *Mistakes Were Made (but not by me): Why We Justify Foolish Beliefs, Bads Decisions, and Hurtful Acts*. Orlando, FL: Harcourt, 2007.

Tchividjian, Tullian. *Glorious Ruin: How Suffering Sets You Free*. Colorado Springs, CO: David C. Cook, 2012.

Tiebout, Harry M., M. D. "The Ego Factors in Surrender in Alcoholism."
http://silkworth.net/tiebout/tiebout_egofactors.html

Vonnegut, Kurt. "The Work to Be Done." *Rolling Stone*, May 28, 1998.

Zahl, Paul F. M. *Grace in Practice: A Theology of Everyday Life*. Grand Rapids, MI: Eerdmans, 2007.

Zahl, Simeon. *Pneumatology and Theology of the Cross in the Preaching of Christoph Friedrich Blumhardt: The Holy Spirit between Wittenberg and Azusa Street*. London, UK: T&T Clark, 2010.

The Book of Common Prayer. New York, NY: The Church Hymnal Corporation, 1979.

Printed in Great Britain
by Amazon